A Gold Miner's Daughter

A Gold Miner's Daughter

Memoirs of a
Mountain Childhood

Shyrle Pedlar Hacker

Johnson Books
Boulder

1470 1971
(L)

Published in the United States by Johnson Books, a division of Johnson Publishing Company, 1880 South 57th Court, Boulder, Colorado 80301.

The following chapters were published in *The Quarterly of the Northeastern Historical Society:* "The Mud Wagon," "Here Where It's Safe," and "The Sugar Bowl."

9   8   7   6   5   4   3   2   1

Cover design by Debra B. Topping
Cover photograph (background) by Gary Hacker

Library of Congress Cataloging-in-Publication Data
Hacker, Shyrle.
    A gold miner's daughter : memoirs of a mountain childhood / Shyrle Pedlar Hacker.
        p.   cm.
    Includes index.
    ISBN 1-55566-178-5 (pbk. : alk. paper)
    1. Hacker, Shyrle—Childhood and youth. 2. Nevada—Biography.
3. Mountain life—Nevada.   I. Title.
CT275.H22A3   1996
979.3'03'092—dc20
[B]   96-32348
                                                                         CIP

Printed in the United States by
Johnson Printing
1880 South 57th Court
Boulder, Colorado 80301

♻ Printed on recycled paper with soy ink

Contents

Acknowledgments vi

His Child, Her Child? October 10, 1915 1
Here, Where It's Safe 21
Words 31
Something Scary Out There 40
1917: Being Different 52
Bull Run 65
The Mud Wagon 75
Spies 80
The Sugar Bowl, 1917 86
Bonds 100
Back to California 108
Selma, California, June 1918 113
Berkeley, Summer 1918 122
The Funeral Game 137
Oakland's Upper Crumbs 146
Truce, November 11, 1918 159
The Little Nest 167
Growing Up in a Changing World, 1921–1926 172
Moving Up 180
Epilogue 188

Index 193

Acknowledgments

First I'd like to thank my children: my son, Gary, for making this book possible by taking time from the tight schedule of a business executive to accompany me to the places in Nevada where I lived as a child. Gary followed the book in its early stages and made editing suggestions and offered needed encouragement.

My daughter, Diane Stevens, author of *Liza's Blue Moon* and *Liza's Star Wish*, read the early drafts countless times, during which our relationship shifted from mother-daughter to writer-writer; that was fun. She and her husband, Dr. Joe Stevens, did the last editing before final submission of the manuscript. I thank Diane for the courage it took to help me in a lifelong struggle to achieve communication on a deeper level.

I am grateful to Howard Hickson and the staff at the Elko Museum for access to the *Elko Independent* and *The Daily Free Press* of 1917–1918. I am indebted to Shawn Richard Hall, assistant director of the Elko Museum, for his courtesy in sending copies of available photos; and to the editorial staff for evaluation of chapters, especially to Wilma Holloway for telephone information.

I would be remiss without thanking my life-long friend Antoine Primeaux and his wife, Ellen. Antoine, historian and author who is engaged in writing a history of Tuscarora, helped me to locate the cabin, still standing since I left it in 1917.

Many libraries and book shops have aided in the research for this book. Thanks to Sally Larkin at Pleasant Hill County Library, to Elizabeth Fuller, and to all the librarians who patiently brought out microfilm copies of newspapers from 1916 through 1924; to Mr. Phillips and Sally Thwaits at Walnut Creek

Library for help in locating books on mining in the early part of the century.

For almost thirty years I've met with a group of writers to read and discuss manuscripts. For encouragement and criticism I'd like to thank my friends: Maggie Alyce Christoff, author of *Something Always Sings*; Maurine Miller, author of *Two Loves for Tina*; John Cambell Bruce (author of *The Golden Door* and *Escape From Alcatraz*); E. B. Stambaugh (author of *The Mantis* and *Shut Eye*); John Plumb, mystery writer and past editor of *Contra Costa Times*; Dorothy Benson, poet-writer and past secretary of California Writer's Club; Phillip and Pat Clucas, writers and critics; and to our more recent members.

My thanks go to a group of Children's Writers in whose sessions I've gleaned invaluable suggestions: to Ginger Wadsworth (author of the biographies *Julie Morgan; architect*, *John Muir* and others) and to Mary Peirano for suggestions and encouragement.

Never could I forget Brian Hayes, my computer genius, who has encouraged the Wiz to try, try again!

And finally, thanks go to my editor, Stephen Topping of Johnson Books, for his enthusiasm when he said "yes"; to Mira Perrizo, managing editor, for endless patience in the final editing; to Laurie Milford for her perceptive copyediting, and to all the gracious people at Johnson Books.

Emotion plucks memory
a passion flower
to be discovered
another day, pressed in
the leaves of a book

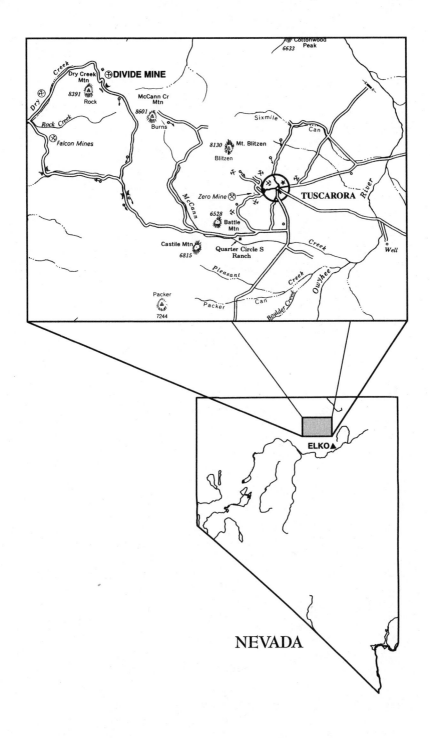

DIVIDE MINE

Creek
Dry Creek
Mtn
8391
Rock
Dry
Rock Creek
Falcon Mines

McCann Cr
Mtn
8601
Burns

Cottonwood
6633   Peak

Sixmile
Can

8130   Mt. Blitzen
Blitzen

River

Zero Mine

TUSCARORA

McCann

6528
Battle
Mtn

Castile Mtn
6815

Quarter Circle S
Ranch

Creek

Well

Pleasant

Packer
7244

Packer

Can

Creek

Boulder Creek

Owyhee

ELKO▲

NEVADA

His Child, Her Child?
October 10, 1915

MOTHER RACED DOWN the railroad tracks, stopping to look in boxcars. Shivering with fear for my cat, Smokey, I stood between two suitcases under the yellow mist of a kerosene lamp on the wall of the railroad station.

Mother was looking to make certain that the cat carrier box had been put aboard. Was Smokey lost? He must be scared. I was scared, too, scared of the great puffing, clanking train with its two engines for the arduous climb over the Sierra. And I was scared because Mother was. Mother didn't want to go. She was afraid something bad would happen. I heard her tell my aunt: "I know I'll regret ever boarding that train, Agnes."

The journey would take us from California, where we had been living with Mother's sister and family on a peach ranch outside the valley town of Selma, to an isolated mountain in northern Nevada. An enthusiastic miner convinced my adventurous father that a fortune of gold awaited us in the Independent Mountains above the mining town *Tuscarora*. No capital was required for this venture—which was well since we had none; one simply staked out a claim, left evidence of pick and shovel intent, then proceeded to the Elko Courthouse to record with witness the location of the claim.

I'm sure Mother would never have consented to move to northern Nevada if I hadn't had whooping cough. Later she told me how Dad tried to persuade her to go, but she'd insisted she was a city girl. All her life she had a love affair with San Francisco. Mother was adamant: Elmer Pedlar would never cart her to some God-forsaken place. Such risky adventure was not for her.

But when my racking cough lingered on, the doctor suggested my parents take me to the mountains. Mountain air was frequently prescribed for lingering coughs.

If the doctor had said, "Take her to the moon," I believe Mother might have invented the first spaceship. I was born two years after Mom lost my sister, Nadine, with croup at six months. Mother's life centered around me, sometimes to my discomfort.

So there we were, an attractive young woman with a bun of abundant reddish brown hair, the near transparent skin of the Scottish Highlands, and a look of defiance in the squint of her small and slightly hooded hazel eyes.

And seated beside her, a skinny, blonde child of five, with frequent coughing seizures. We were on our way to the isolated foothills of Northeast Nevada.

Many times I heard Mother describe that train car. It was a time when trains were considered a remarkable way to travel. They were patronized, except in cases of necessity such as ours, by the wealthy. The poor man traveled by horse, buckboard, or resorted to the slower and bumpier stagecoach.

Mother told me of the dazzling fittings of the cars: of red and green velvet covered seats, of gleaming brass, and the dark brilliance of oiled wood.

~~~~~~~

The coach grows extremely cold. The window ices over. Snow blows down the chimney, and the iron stove in the front of the car smokes. A violent coughing spell seizes me. I feel Mother's cool hand on my head. Her voice reassures me and I must have fallen asleep.

Dad had sent us the railroad tickets to Elko, Nevada. From there, we were to take the mud wagon, a smaller version of the stagecoach, to Tuscarora, where he would meet us with the buckboard.

The population of Tuscarora was around 300 at the time we arrived. It had taken nearly eight hours to drive forty miles from Elko on the old dirt road through sagebrush that stretched to ocean horizons. Every eight miles the small stagecoach stopped to change horses at such places as Reed Station, Eagle Rock, Twin Bridges, or one of the houses that offered hospitality—food and lodging if required, hay for horses, beer or bourbon for thirsty travelers.

It is not difficult to imagine Mother's dismay when she learned we were nearing our destination.

The weathered sign, *Tuscarora*, stood on a fence post with white peeling paint to indicate a dirt road taking off between sage and cow brush. The town's shacks and dilapidated buildings sprawled across the ankle of Mount Blitzen. On approaching this ghost town from the Elko Road, the first eye-catcher was the cemetery. Here time, weather, and weeds intruded to leave only sections of a once-white picket fence, mounds of unidentified graves among a few scattered stone markers, and a wooden cross wind-beaten until its once-stalwart arms wavered between earth and heaven.

Tuscarora followed the course of most western towns engendered by the rumor of gold. In 1867 a mining district was formed, and by 1875 an outfit called Young American Company had laid out a town site and was selling lots on all property not already claimed by squatters. When the Grand Prize Mine made a first shipment of refined bullion—seven bars valued at $11,126 (today the worth would surpass $300,000)—scores of big rigs arrived and stage coaches brought in more than fifty people a day. The boom years reached a peak in 1880; from then on production slowed, mines closed, and the population dropped from 5,000 to 3,500 and continued to spiral downward.

On that day in the fall of 1915, did I say 300 people were left in town? Well maybe . . . could be a couple of hundred were still scratching away at mines somewhere in the vicinity and planning to winter in Tuscarora.

Having witnessed subsequent arrivals of the stage coach, I don't find it difficult to picture ours.

Six or eight men—unemployed miners and the town's business men—would have awaited the arrival of the stage, the big event of the day; the men grouped together on the wooden sidewalk in front of the small post office.

Dad waited for us. He'd driven over the mountain in his buckboard with two horses, Dolly and Jerky. Dad embraced Mother, ignoring her tight lips, and lifted out his sleeping five-year-old.

"My wife, Tess, boys," he would sing out with hearty congeniality. "And this is my little girl, Shirley."

The men would look shy and shuffle their feet. A few might mutter acknowledgments to Mother, then turn with apparent relief to Dad.

"So this is your family, huh Ped? You been waitin' a long time."

There might have been some fear of Mother. No one would kid with her. Awed by an apparent fury, as well as her fair-skinned beauty in a land of sun-baked women, these men would turn to Dad. He was one of them.

Dad must have transferred us into a buckboard behind Dolly and Jerky. It is just as well that I do not recollect what Mother had to say when they were alone. And if she vented her wrath at the first sight of Tuscarora, then, after they circled the steep road around Mount Blitzen to drive 12 miles over dirt roads, over no roads at all, past six or eight scattered cabins and Buck Horn's Saloon and Post Office, finally to arrive at an isolated cabin in a sea of blowing sage, there is little doubt that Mother's fury echoed the battle cries of her Highland Scottish ancestry, those McDonald warlords.

In a meadow by a mountain stream, the one-room cabin with a lean-to awaited our arrival. Likely left by some disappointed miner from the 1880 boom, the cabin had been reinforced by Dad and his partner, Huddleson—known as Hud. Chicken wire covered the tar paper and laths, the wire staked to the ground to defy fierce winds in that high mountain country.

Tin cans, mostly empty coal oil cans, had been flattened and nailed to the roof or siding to provide weather stripping. The men added a lean-to on the north side for my cot.

The lean-to housed an iron cooking stove and a small chest of drawers beside my bed. The back wall of the lean-to served as cupboard space with a "cooler" opening to the outside for storage of wild game and trout. During the winter, snow covered the back of the "cooler," lending attributes of the latest model freezer from G.E.

The outhouse was located about 30 yards behind the cabin, so the wind wafting the scent lost none of its pith. During winter, the temperature might provide incentive for an Olympic trainer.

Mother never settled in. From the moment we arrived, she must have set her wily mind on seeking some way to escape. Perhaps she would look at her child grown thin and delicate from the long bout with whooping cough and gather fortitude to wait a little longer. I doubt if any prisoner counted days and planned for parole more constantly than Mother.

For me, here in this isolated wilderness I would spend the most impressionable years of my childhood. I would come to love nature and animals. Dad showed me how to gather pine nuts to feed the squirrels and chipmunks. Often a chipmunk rode on my shoulder and chattered to me. I named them and it puzzled my parents how I could tell them apart. I fed the robins bread crumbs and soon I had several pet birds: a robin named Red and one named Heidi. When the quail gathered around the cabin door, scolding for crumbs, Mom said, "Your chickens are waiting to be fed." Several snowshoe rabbits became pets. They liked carrot tops and peelings, and I loved to hold and cuddle the white baby bunnies.

Through a splendid loneliness I sensed myself as part of an interconnecting web of all living things. If this was the fertile soil for creativity, solitude was the path to the garden.

Story books had taught me that enchanted places are never perfect. On the dark side, I could not escape my parents' quarreling. Anger in their voices frightened me. That anger hung over our heads like some demon out of Grimms' scary *Fairy Tales*.

Most of the time I was *her* child. Some of the time I was *his*. Never was I—*their* child. And when the three of us were together there was within me a disturbed feeling of divided loyalty not yet defined.

～～

"I'm going to buy some kind of curtains for these windows," Mother announced, looking around at the unfinished walls of the cabin with a glint of hatred in her deep-set hazel eyes. "And I don't care whether we can afford it or not!"

Dad's expression would be amused and tolerant. A big man, he had a large head with brown curly hair, receding now in his late forties to further widen a high forehead.

"Never could understand why people cut holes in houses to let in light and air then hang rags over them. Would seem they defeat the purpose, Tereda." Tereda was a pet name. "You won't need curtains. No one looks in on us here except a stray coyote."

Mother got curtains. Blue dotted muslin from the Sears Catalog.

As Dad often said, "Tereda rules the roost." His philosophical view of life. Her driving ambition.

"You have no responsibility, Elmer Pedlar. You're utterly selfish. My child deserves a decent home and she's going to have it. If I have to manage it alone, I will!"

And Dad would say, "Come, sit on the riverbank with me and listen to a robin. Anything that anyone could want is right here."

Slowly I became aware that the conflict between my parents was unsolvable. At some later time I recognized I had inherited the warring factors in each parent so that an inner truce would never be possible.

The conflict may have lain in the slope of the land as well, for we'd arrived at a place called The Divide. Here, high in the mountains, a rain drop or a trickling stream has a choice of flowing south to the Humboldt Sink or running northwest into the Pacific Ocean.

Life does not begin with birth. Our lives are part of a flow of generations into which we fall like snowflakes at some time in history.

Mother's family genes reached back far beyond the potato farmers driven from Ireland by famine to sail for America, far beyond the McDonald warlords, beyond invading tribes of Saxons or Celts, beyond, beyond . . .

Dad's family fished off the rocky coast of Penzance on England's Cornish coast. And before that? Perhaps, pirates? Surely, Celts . . .

History's stream, winding through this tiny northeastern corner of Nevada, preceded the arrival of our creaking buckboard into a time beyond man's knowledge. Here, long before the fur traders and trappers came, Paiute and Goshute Indians rode these highlands hunting buffalo and elk. With the flow of generations in the stream of history, I like to think I was washed up on the banks of Jack's Creek at The Divide or farther north from the Bull Run River. Actually my birth took place in San Francisco, but it was on The Sandy Shore where I was born into awareness.

The Sandy Shore. Somewhere there is an oval patch of riverbank, hidden away by a dense growth of cottonwoods, sage, and pussy willow. Somewhere there is a phantom realm of creativity where the life of my imagination began. It may be at The Divide or at Bull Run. Likely at both. It was there on the Sandy Shore where I learned deceit.

In the early mornings Mother arranges a place for me on the bank among my dolls and books, while she goes fishing. As soon as she is out of sight around the bend in the river, I drop the book or doll she had given me to play with. I gather folds of my faded cotton skirt in two fists—what I thought of as The Wad. As I squeeze the gathered folds of my dress, a sensuous excitement grips me. It is the same feeling I've experienced many times since when an idea sends me dashing to the typewriter.

I squeeze The Wad, shake it slowly at first, and then faster and faster as I warm up. A mountain silence encircles my solitude, broken only by the hum of insects or occasional bird talk. To escape loneliness, my thoughts burrow into that silence that is deep as Dad's tunnels. There I strike a rich vein and stories float out of the air. An occasional griffin floats past. Smokey, my constant companion, sits beside me and works her paws up and down on my leg so I wonder what cat stories she tells. The Sandy Shore. I can feel the damp sand under my bottom. I can smell sage and the river. Again I experience the awesome sensation of being watched by millions of insect eyes. What must insects think of this huge body of a child? One of their tribe sounds a tick-tick-tick. Insect time. Much more rapid than human time. Could an insect live a lifetime in an hour?

Of all the stories that reeled through my brain during the years in that lost landscape, the earliest one concerned a remarkable elephant. Having never been to a zoo, I had only seen pictures of elephants. The one in my fantasy was an awesome size. I see him now, his great head towering above the pine trees, trunk swinging. On his side, an invisible door which opens at my command. A ladder drops and, with Smokey in my arms, I climb up and enter. Inside his thick hide, a panel of commands awaits my wishes. At the press of a button, my Elephant Mobile can walk, run, fly, or swim.

It is a puzzle how this panel, much like a computer or a control panel in a plane, entered a child's imagination at that time. This story must have been a serial for I have vague recollections of many adventures: I rescued animals from floods, fires and cruel owners until that elephant interior must have resembled Noah's Ark.

It might have been of interest to Jung that these stories centered around a dream of power. Superchild acquires elephant hide to conquer all enemies. Times there have been when I wished I'd preserved that hide! The power-loving child has never departed. Sometimes I recognize her.

Mother never tells me not to pursue the Muse in this unconventional way. She simply refuses to recognize that a child of hers could indulge in such peculiar behavior. I feel the burning guilt of her disapproval.

When I look up, Mother stands there in the river watching me. Her skirts are tucked inside her bloomers while the water rushes past her high-topped boots. She holds a fishing rod and the line stretches taut on a rebuking current. I glimpse a worried frown for a moment before Mother conceals it.

It has taken me little time to learn adult hypocrisy. Quickly I release The Wad, smooth out the wrinkles in my skirt, and grab my doll.

"Betty Maria," I scold, spanking her, "You're a bad girl."

Mother smiles approval. But could I guess that beating a doll was acceptable behavior and story telling in my fashion was not?

She calls brightly, "Would you like to fish with me for awhile?"

Distractions. Always she offers distractions. Without words she tells me I'm doing something "not nice." Like picking my nose.

For years I shaped The Wad out of whatever material was on hand—a piece of clothing, a corner of a bed sheet, a towel. Always with guilt like a criminal in hiding, I would slip away to a solitary spot to release the growing pressure of stories needing to be told. At what age I substituted The Word for The Wad, I don't remember. The written word, that is.

Mother took my hand and squeezed it warmly while we went back to the cabin with the fish she'd caught strung on a branch. I sensed a vast and lonely distance between us—that endless prairie of guilt. I longed to please her. I saw myself, a strange child who did odd things, and I was dreadfully sorry but I couldn't stop telling my stories. Mother and I were different and the knowledge hurt because I loved her so much and wanted to be like her. Deep down I knew that on that day I was not her child.

How often do you read the phrase, "I had an enchanted childhood"? Does anyone actually have an enchanted childhood? Enchanted moments would be more accurate. Such moments may loom up out of the mist of memory to upset those fragile boundaries of human calendars, clocks, and, sometimes, geography.

In my enchanted moments, I entertained myself with stories because I never knew what was coming next, but sometimes I whispered to an imaginary playmate Nadine—the name of my sister who died in infancy.

The times with Dad held enchantment, too. On an October day Dad and I went on one of our walks through the woods. He always carried a rifle, but only recently had I become aware of the gun. Our conversation may have gone something like this:

"Why do you always bring a gun?" I asked.

"You never know what you'll run into, Turk." Dad never called anyone by a given name. The nick-name Turk was suggested by a beaver turban Mom had made for me. Dad remarked that I looked like a little Turk and the name stuck.

"Coyotes usually keep their distance," he explained, "but you can't rely on wolves or bears. Me thinks it's the better part of wisdom to be prepared."

"Are wolves and bears—bad then?"

Dad waited a long time to answer. Finally he said, "The question, Little Turk, of what's good or bad is one every man must decide for himself. If something hurts you or threatens you, you'll be inclined to think of that thing as—bad. But that may be only the way you see it, understand? Now in the case of the wolves, they may be hunting because they're hungry and from their viewpoint you look like a juicy steak."

"Why can't they eat bark from the trees like the beaver?"

"Because the Creator made them carnivorous rather than herbivorous animals. That means they have sharp teeth and prefer flesh to vegetation."

In silence I considered that for some time. Daddy always shared wiggly-worm words with me, words that told me he considered me his equal.

"Did God mean for his creatures to kill each other?" I felt certain He hadn't. Mother had taught me to say, "God is good," in my prayers. How could a good God get his world mixed up like that?

"Nature, it would appear, attempts to keep a balance in the world. If some animals didn't destroy others, the forest would be overrun. Then many would starve."

I tried to come to understand this. Was Nature something that took care of the world when God was busy elsewhere?

"But why—why didn't God just make less animals?"

"All creatures, it would appear, were left to re-create themselves. They are born with instinct to hunt and kill for food."

I had heard the coyotes howl in the night.

"Poor coyotes and wolves," I murmured. "If they weren't hungry they wouldn't be our enemies, would they?"

Twigs and dry leaves crackled under our feet. A hot wind carried the smell of dry sage. I wound my fingers around Dad's maimed hand. Three fingers on his left hand had been cut off at the second knuckle in a boxcar accident when Dad was working as a brakeman. I liked to rub the rounded finger stumps on his calloused hand.

"Are the Huns hungry?" I must have been thinking of conversations between my parents after letters about the Germans arrived from her sisters, my Aunt Kitty and Aunt Williford. "Is that why they're called—Huns?"

Dad chuckled. He was a history buff and explained that the term Hun referred to Asiatic people led by a man, called Attila. Knowing Dad, he must have talked for a long time about the invasion of eastern and central Europe in the 4th and 5th centuries. I remember little of this conversation except that "Hun" had become a hateful term for German soldiers. I continued to connect the word with hunger.

"Are the Huns our enemies?"

"Well, that's what we're being led to believe at the moment." Dad looked intently into the distance as if he saw something there. "Someday, perhaps in your lifetime, people will refuse to have enemies set up for them to hate and kill."

I looked up at my father's whiskered chin. He shaved once a week at Mother's insistance. Sometimes I was awed at how high up his head was from mine. It had taken him a long, long time to grow so tall and in that time I guessed he had learned everything. I hoped when I'd grown tall I might be wise and perfect as my Dad.

On that day I was his child.

~~~

Some of this conversation may have been repeated later to Mother and thus impressed on my memory. Shut away as we were from daily news or human gossip, subjects for conversation were few. I, being an only child, provided a great deal of this material and often heard my remarks repeated. Dad's opinion on these subjects I knew from repetition over the years.

~~~

Mother washed clothes outside. She packed buckets of water up from Jack's Creek, a branch of Owyhee River. On the brick fire pit, she heated the water. The soapy clothes finally went back to the river for rinsing.

Sometimes she took the washboard and soap to do all the washing in the river, but Mother was a great one for boiling clothes at least once a month. In the winter she used the old iron stove inside my lean-to, but she didn't like to overheat the cabin during summer. The floor ventilating system kept it cool.

When the cabin was built, the floor boards were cut too short, so they lacked a few inches in meeting the walls. In the winter, twisted newspapers shut off these "vents"; our inexpensive air conditioner was hardly a decorator's dream.

On the ground, not far from the wash tub, I was building an Indian village with sticks. Dad had promised to take me to see an Indian village on the Duck Valley Indian Reservation, which lay a short distance to the north, on the Nevada-Idaho border.

Smokey believed I was playing a game with him and kept snatching at my sticks.

Then something caused me to look up at the pile of rocks near the brick fire pit. Dad used these rocks to cook partridge, sage hens, mud hens, and grouse, Indian fashion. The fowl, feathers and all, were covered with clay from the river bank, buried in a pit under hot rocks, and cooked for hours. Feathers came off with the clay, leaving the birds tender and juicy.

Taken from the mines, some of these rocks contained fool's gold that glinted in the blazing sun. My eye caught something move from underneath the rock pile. A large snake slithered out not more than eight feet from where I sat.

I screamed. It was automatic. The oneness I felt with wild creatures and birds did not include Eve's tempter. From these critters, I'd been warned to keep my distance. Rattlers were plentiful in the desert terrain.

Mother whirled at my scream, snatched me, and carried me into the cabin. There I was soothed and given a graham cracker. Mother's voice trembled. Then I remembered Smokey, and Mother ran out to get him. The snake was gone, she told me, I was safe. But when she went to finish hanging out clothes, I chose to stay on top of the table, Smokey gripped in my arms.

Then, a few moments after she left, a snake's head slowly rose from between the opposite wall and the floor. It had come to get me. The head wavered for a second while I watched, frozen. It looked directly at me. I screamed, or thought I did, for it turned out to be one of those dream-screams that can't escape. The snake swayed another moment, then pulled back.

Now the screams came as quickly as I could catch my breath. Mother rushed in, held me, tried to soothe me, but I couldn't stop. Finally she gripped my shoulders and shook me. "Stop that, Shirley, this instant!"

The screams subsided but I refused to get off the table. Mother twisted newspapers and filled the gaps in the floor. Before she went out again she took a hoe off its nail on the cabin wall. When she returned her face was white as the snowshoe bunny.

"The snake won't bother you again. It's dead." Her voice told me she shared my fear of the slithery thing.

I was never convinced that snake was dead. He was my enemy

and for the rest of my life I expected that, at some unguarded moment, he would find me.

That day I recognized Mother as my protector against the dangers of the world. She could kill snakes, do anything. A warm rush of love and gratitude washed over me.

I was her child.

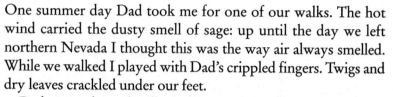

One summer day Dad took me for one of our walks. The hot wind carried the dusty smell of sage: up until the day we left northern Nevada I thought this was the way air always smelled. While we walked I played with Dad's crippled fingers. Twigs and dry leaves crackled under our feet.

Dad stopped on a knoll overlooking a short stretch of flatland before the roll of hills. He withdrew his hand from mine to signal a warning for me to be quiet. Then I saw the young deer on top of the knoll across from us. He had that look of having paused between leaps, and stood listening and watchful. Probably he had caught our scent.

My feelings reached out to communicate. I was bonded to him, as with the rabbits and chipmunks and other wild creatures. Animals communicated without words. The message—we belong to the same family—passed between us on the breeze. I gazed from his velvet horns to his short, white tail.

I did not see Dad lift the gun. I jerked, then screamed as the sound of the blast ripped through me. The young deer staggered a step, crumpled, and fell.

I stared at the my father in horror. It was unbelievable that my perfect father was a cruel man. Bad. He had betrayed me. "How could you do that?" I screamed at him. "You killed him! He didn't do anything to us and you—!"

Dad dropped the gun. I will never forget the look on his face.

I thought he was about to cry. He knelt to put his arms around me. I backed away from him, sobbing.

He tried to explain that we would be hungry if he didn't put in a supply of food for next winter. Of course I knew there were meat and fowl in the cabinet adjoining my room, but I'd never considered how they got there. The cabinet opened from both inside and out—except when the cabin wall was covered with snow. Never before had I been with Dad when he hunted.

Now all I could see were the trustful eyes of the young buck. It was as though someone had unravelled rows of stitches in the wrapper that bound us safely together—all of us—the deer, Dad, and me.

When the deer fell my father went down, too. If I couldn't trust my own father to do what was good, then who was there? The world was all mixed up. I wanted so much to understand what was bad and what was good.

In silence we trudged back to the cabin, the young buck over Dad's shoulder. I avoided looking at it, even though I couldn't see through tears.

Mother was furious at Dad, too. But for a wrong reason.

"You should have known better than to shoot before the child," she cried, holding me against her.

I couldn't believe this. Even my mother approved of Dad killing the deer as long as I didn't see him do it!

Dad said something about "the buck—such a good shot—aimed before I thought."

"She's got to grow up sometime, Tereda," he insisted. "You can't go on keeping facts from her. She's got to learn now that life isn't always pleasant, or she's going to be badly hurt someday." He tried to meet my eyes but I refused to look at him.

"The Turk understands," he said, "that I only shoot to feed my family, same as the wolves and coyotes and—"

There was a question in his voice. I knew he shared my love for animals. Then how could he—?

I couldn't understand. When I was in bed that night on the single cot in the lean-to, I still felt the deer's pain and my father's treachery.

When Mother came to hear prayers, I asked her why we couldn't eat plants and the bark of trees as the beaver do.

She brushed my hair back off my forehead and kissed me.

Sometimes when she watched me closely like this, I felt she was looking into my head, checking my thoughts. If she could put a restraining hand across them in the way she protected my eyes, she would.

She didn't try always to answer my questions the way Dad did. "Say your prayers now, darling, and go to sleep."

The prayer she'd taught me was a simple one. "Heavenly Father, hear my prayer. Keep me always in your care . . ." There was no mention of death.

When weather permitted, Dad went outdoors to smoke while I said prayers. I never asked him to listen because somewhere in my unexamined thoughts, I knew prayers were of no interest to him. Sometimes I wondered if Dad wasn't interested, how God could be.

That night I hoped He was, as I had something important to say to Him. After a soft Amen, I added, "Bless Mother and Dad and Smokey and the wild creatures. And, please God, take better care of your creatures and stop them from hurting one another. Amen."

I didn't understand my parents. They didn't understand me. I was alone and it was a lonely alone. I was no one's child.

Mother grew up on a sheep ranch in a place called the Estrella, near Paso Robles, California. She was Mary Theresa—called Tess—one of fourteen children, seven girls and seven boys in a

Catholic family. Her mother, a frail Irish woman, had the manner, when I knew her, of having given up long ago. Mom's father, an intelligent, well-read Scotsman who liked his whiskey, returned from jaunts to town just long enough to get his wife, Mary, pregnant again—so it seemed to Tess. She once told me how she would listen to bed springs in her parents' room at night and clench her fists in fury, half in sympathy for her fragile and weary mother, half for herself who would shoulder the burden of caring for yet another baby. Once she told me it was her mother's frequent pregnancies that had turnd her and all her sisters away from the Catholic faith.

Beyond all else she longed to go to school, but work at home interfered with her attendance at the small schoolhouse started by her father and supported by a few other ranchers. Laughlin McDonald was a strong believer in education for girls as well as boys. He provided the school. If his virility interfered with his belief, there could be no question of priorities. He chose not to notice girls at home washing floors or scrubbing at diaper stains on a washboard during school hours.

At twenty, after breaking up with her farm boy sweetheart, the great love of her life, Tess went on the road selling Royal Baking Powder. Such a job for a young woman in those early years of the twentieth century provides evidence to her independence and complete disregard for what others might think. In Gilroy, California—where he was born—she met Elmer Ellsworth Pedlar, a big, burly outdoorsman who worked for the Fish and Game Commission. She married him in Benicia, California, in 1907. She was twenty-one; Dad, over twenty years her senior.

I've often wondered about the attraction between them. Mother was said to have been a beauty with her mass of auburn hair and fair skin. It is easy to imagine Dad's attraction for this beautiful and naive farm girl.

Why did she decide to marry this older man? She must have been attracted by his appearance, brilliant mind, and sense of humor. I can picture him taking her to dinner and entertaining her with amusing stories of his travel and quotes from Shakespeare.

The Pedlar family, many of whom were writers, librarians, and musicians, occupied a more enviable rung on the social ladder, if a less prosperous one, than the sheep ranchers. Dad had one sister, Minnie. His parents, proud of his scholastic honors, sent him off to the University of California expecting him to become a lawyer. Elmer found law books impossibly dull and took off for adventures in his youth. He traveled in Italy and Mexico, where he learned Spanish and worked off-and-on jobs when necessity demanded. He was a carpenter, a brakeman on the Southern Pacific, a chef in a short-order cafe, and sold everything from brushes to sheet music. Fluent in Spanish, he taught English in Mexican schools.

When he was thirty Dad married a woman slightly older than himself. The only thing I knew about this marriage was that Mother once told me that she and Dad used to laugh together about his first wife, who Dad described as a cold and precise woman.

Dad, a young romantic at the time, was appalled when she told him that they could have sex only on Friday nights. He admitted to Mom that he had been "utterly turned off" when his bride appeared in her long flannel nightgown on a Friday night. She wore a night cap and carried a douche bag.

Soon Dad made it a point not to be home on Friday nights.

After two years of marriage, this wife took their infant daughter and left. Dad was served with divorce papers and never saw his family again. I often wished I could have known my stepsister, Dolores.

Dad never spoke of this daughter unless I questioned him. A constant reader, he continued—even after his marriage to Mom—to write long letters, discussing books and world affairs, to teachers and other female friends he'd met on his travels. This must have been painful to Mom. Was he insensitive to her feelings of inferiority? This is difficult to believe for he was a sensitive man. Perhaps he tried to discuss his interests with her and in her burning anger, she rejected him. I believe he was as lonely as Mother and had an inner conflict as great. A philosopher, he claimed to be an agnostic. One side of him needed to live close to nature and valued freedom and solitude; yet he had many friends and never ceased to hunger after intellectual stimulation. A charmer, raconteur, adventurer, and delightful companion, he was generous to a fault with everyone except Mother. With her, he was a selfish man.

It must have been Mom's lack of schooling that left her with a deep sense of inferiority, although she often impressed people as being overly confident. Growing up on a sheep ranch failed to provide any social status. Perhaps she resented Dad for these privileges. Behind her desire to return to California was a determination to get me into good schools and to provide an acceptable home.

So there they were. Different as the tranquil woods and striving city they represented. Each intent on a different goal. Each armed for battle.

Here Where It's Safe

WE HAD BEEN WARNED by other miners not to remain at the Divide Mining District through that winter of 1916. Because of the severity of the weather, most miners, especially those with families, wintered in Tuscarora about twelve miles down the mountain.

It was not by choice that we prepared to spend the winter in our one-room cabin with the lean-to. The first winter we'd rented in Tuscarora. But, by 1916, we could no longer afford lodging.

I was going on seven and until that winter had never been fully aware of what my mother's life must have been like. She was no more than thirty, while Dad was past fifty. However, she was imbued with the pioneer spirit.

"We'll make do," she often said.

We did. Along with my friends the squirrels and chipmunks we prepared, or so we thought, for the months ahead. We stuffed the cracks between floor and walls with newspapers and filled the huge fuel box with cottonwood and dried sage for kindling.

Disregarding my love for animals, Mother lined my wool coat with rabbit skins and made the beaver-skin turban.

A stack of boxes along an inside wall of the cabin contained canned vegetables and fruit. I overheard many discussions over the venison, duck, and trout packed under snow and ice in our "freezer," one of two inside-outside cabinets built on the rear of the cabin, the second cabinet, a woodbox. Extra wood, stacked outside the cabin, was covered with canvas. Would the supplies last until spring?

Mom and Dad tried to guess when they might expect the spring thaw that would make it safe to drive the twelve miles down the grade for supplies. Twelve miles, given the road conditions and pace of a horse-driven buckboard in a storm, could take as long as three or even four hours.

For me the hours, like falling snow, went on and on divided by darkness and light with the darkest hours changing only by degree. On the calendar our icy fingers marked out the days—days that crept across the page to a week, and finally, a month. Sometimes the snow blew in flurries; sometimes turning to hail, it pelted down on the cabin roof.

I would rub a peeking space on the window pane and look up at glistening icicles decorating our roof or gaze at a white world broken only by a scattering of frosted sagebrush until snow concealed all. Farther across the valley, branches of pine drooped beneath their heavy burden and I thought of the buried robins' homes, imagining that bird song, too, was frozen in the silence. By January snow threatened to bury our home. Every few hours Mom or Dad went out with a shovel to clear the path from our door to the outhouse and to the shelter for the animals. Each time they would bring in a supply of wood to dry out for the next day. For me it often seemed that time like everything else had frozen to a stop. There we were, our lives suspended in this small space with a constant smell of dry sage burning in the iron stove. I had no solitary place to escape into my alternate world. Mother wrote to her sister for books to read to me. I guess she may have hoped to wean me from The Wad. Even though I missed the imagination games I played on The Sandy Shore, I loved hearing the adventures of *Heidi* that winter. The only sad thing was knowing the book would end and that my new friend, Heidi, would vanish.

Locked together in the one-room-plus cabin, my parents must have worn on each other's nerves for they constantly bickered and quarreled. I couldn't shut out the unhappy voices. How I longed for spring to set me free.

At night I heard the sorrowful howl of a coyote and the angry wind roaring as it whipped across the mountain.

In the mornings, wrapped in a blanket, I studied under a kerosene lamp that flashed strange shadows on the wall where the guns hung. Sometimes, bundled in scarves and my rabbit-lined coat, I went with Mother to bring in fuel or to race down a newly shoveled path to the outhouse. Other times I went with Dad to the stable to feed and supply dry blankets to Dolly, the mare, and Minniehaha, our burro. Between meals, a clutter of books, magazines, and paper dolls filled the table. Mother read to me. I played with Smokey but missed the chipmunks who rode on my shoulder and my imaginary playmates who waited down at The Sandy Shore. Soon the color of those days blended until all our mundane activities ran together to leave only the memory of a single scene like an impressionist painting on a post card: icicles hanging from an isolated cabin, whites blending into creeping shadows.

One day I turned from the window to watch Dad pack the battered brown suitcase. "Are you going away, Daddy?"

"Just my usual trip down the mountain, Turk. I'll be back day after tomorrow. Bring you some candy."

"Thought I'd better make it now," he told Mother, "while the storm has let up a bit. We need to stock up on supplies. Cupboard's as bare as a jay bird's shins."

Huddleson, Dad's partner, lived alone in a cabin about two miles across the valley near The Divide. Every winter he put runners on his wagon to turn it into a sled. For the trip down the mountain, Hud and Dad hitched Dolly up with Hud's horse, Jerky.

Reassured that Dad would return, I helped Mom break holes in the ice so we could fish in the river. Shivering, while we waited to get a bite, I recited multiplication tables. Mom insisted on giving me daily lessons.

But that day fish weren't biting.

"Too many fishermen upstream," Mom said, and the frown twins puckered her forehead.

The day Dad was supposed to return another storm arrived. The cabin shook with the violent winds and the old stove smoked and failed to keep us warm. My fingers were blue and stiff as I helped Mom twist newspaper and stuff the cracks and knotholes. Hail, like tiny snowballs, beat on the window and sounded like a hollow drum on the roof. Mother spent a lot of time at the window, squinting to see down the road. I asked her many questions. Why didn't Daddy come? Had his wagon gone off the side of the mountain into a snowdrift? What would happen to us if he didn't come back?

"It will be all right," she kept telling me. "Don't worry."

I couldn't help but worry when she did.

One morning I woke up early to find the cabin empty. The storm had subsided. I scrambled out of the double bed that I'd shared with Mom to run barefoot to the door in my flannel nightgown. Out there in the snow, about thirty feet from where I stood, a small snowshoe bunny merged into the landscape. Often in the early summer I had watched these rabbits wiggle and kick to remove their winter pelt. Now I wished I had carrot tops for Bonnie Bunny; then I saw Mother. A scream rose in my throat. Dressed in her bulky beaver with the snow halfway up her high boots, she aimed a rifle at Bonnie Bunny.

My scream startled both the rabbit and Mom. She lowered the gun and the frightened rabbit quickly disappeared. I looked at her as if I'd never seen her before. I shouted and it must have been something like, "You were going to shoot it! How could you?"

As she came into the cabin, her face told me something was terribly wrong. Her pretty mouth was tucked in until she had no lips at all.

With a heavy sigh she hung the gun on the wall.

"You know I wouldn't shoot a bunny unless it was necessary," she said, and sat down in the rocker. Then she told me we were running out of food. "Your father should have been back a week ago with supplies. With this last storm the road may be closed.

We'll manage somehow," she said as I climbed into her lap.

"You mean we could starve?" I'd heard about people who had starved before supplies could reach them.

"Don't worry," she said. "I'll think of something."

"Couldn't we catch fish?"

Why fish were immune to my sympathy, I don't know.

"Ice on the river is too heavy to break through. Anyway I doubt if they're biting."

I wasn't too worried. Mother was resourceful and she'd promised to think of something.

What she decided seemed a good idea at the time. We saddled Minniehaha, bundled up in our snow clothes, and started up the zig-zag trail to the old Robinson house.

The Robinson brothers used to come in the summer to do a little mining and a great deal of hunting and fishing. I never knew if they owned the clapboard house with the yellow peeling paint that stood up there alone on the top of the mountain. I thought of it as the castle. Likely it was three or four rooms at the most. Compared to our shanty it was huge.

We became acquainted with the Robinson brothers the summer when Ben shot Fritz, one of my squirrels. When Ben saw me crying and realized the squirrel was a pet he tried to make amends. I was inconsolable. So he built the chipmunk cage with the tiny ferris wheel and after I had extracted his promise never to shoot another squirrel, we became friends. Promptly I asked Dad to remove the door from the cage so my wild friends could come and go as they wished. The cage was seldom empty. The Robinson boys, and sometimes Buck Horn, brought peanuts for me to feed to the squirrels and chipmunks.

At the end of each summer Ben and his brother boarded up the house with the peeling yellow paint and returned to the city.

I must have reminded Mother that the house would be locked and boarded up, for I remember the shock of her words: "We are going to break in."

I had been strictly raised to "be a good girl." Now my own mother proposed to break into someone else's house! I guessed we were going to get into bad trouble. Maybe go to jail. I'd never been so frightened.

It was a long, long way up the zig-zag trail. Sometimes I sat on top of the pack boxes that Mother had tied on with rope to Haha's sides. Even in my fur-pieced coat and high beaver hat, I was cold. My breath made smoke. I was a sultan riding an elephant and smoking a funny pipe. But even the flow of my stories was frozen. My eyes cried cold tears.

Mother suggested I might keep warmer if I walked. Our feet crunched on the icy path. A brave blue jay flew from tree to tree, scolding. We walked into the wind that came in gusts to lift the snow from the bank into poufs like powder. Wind stung my face. Except for our footsteps and the screech of the jay, the world was wrapped in a white tissue silence. The sky hung low and heavy over trees packed with snow.

I was troubled and my stomach growled after our meager meal of tea and hardtack. The latter was a coarse unleavened bread that I had to dip into hot tea before I could bite it off. Hardtack, it was said, lasted forever and so it was valued by miners in this unreliable country where supplies might suddenly be cut off. It was always on Dad's grocery list.

I began to sense Mother's growing fear. She had the far-away look and didn't hear me when I spoke to her. To escape the terror of what was going to happen to us, I turned my thoughts to happy times:

Bright days. The zig-zag trail is dusty under bare feet. Green trees spring to life with bird song, bird chatter. Pebbles skip along with the touch of a toe. I think of the smell of pine and sage and green clover and the taste of water trickling down over the rocks where we'd often stopped to fill a tin cup. In summer, water tastes thin and cool as the high mountain air.

But now I scrunched my body to draw away from the wind. The house on top of the mountain remained far, far away. By the time we finally reached the Big House my teeth chattered, not because I was shaky cold but because I was shaky scared. Mother really meant what she'd said about breaking in. She started at once knocking off icicles in front of a window and tugging at the boards nailed over the pane. Soon her hands were bleeding from the cold. Across the back of her hand the skin was split from a stove burn that never healed.

I no longer knew if my tears were cold ones or sad ones. I tried to help her but my fingers hurt even through my mittens and she gave me a stick to break icicles.

When the boards were off, Mother found a big rock. When I saw what she was going to do I yelled at her to stop. Had she lost her mind?

"Mom, we'll go to jail."

"No, we won't, darling." The Robinson boys, she explained, would understand that we must eat. We would repay them for everything we took.

I had always suspected that my mother could do anything she had to do. I guessed it the day she killed the rattlesnake. But now I knew it.

She lifted me in through the hole in the window, warning me to be careful of shattered glass. I could hear the wind, stronger up here on the top of the mountain, more frightening as it whipped the trees and I could hear my heart but the empty rooms held only scary silence and a musty smell. The cupboards were almost empty. I handed cans of milk, half a can of cocoa, and coffee out to Mother, who packed the gear on Haha's sides. Mother smiled when I found a can of corned beef although I'd never liked it. We were doing something bad. What would happen to us?

After she'd lifted me out, I asked, "Aren't you going to board up their window?"

"I have no tools. Dad or Huddleson will have to come and do it when they get back."

Mother was silent on the long trip down the mountain. I guessed she was awfully worried or awfully angry at Daddy. He couldn't help it if storms closed the roads, could he? I gave up trying to talk to her. Maybe she didn't want to talk because the cold hurt your teeth too much when you opened your mouth.

When we got back to the cabin I helped bring in the damp sage brush, which produced more smoke than warmth from the wood stove. I continued to shiver until Mother lit the oil burner that she usually used only for baths. She rubbed my toes and fingers briskly with snow, so I wouldn't get chilblain, she said.

For supper the hot chocolate tasted wonderful. Even the slice of corned beef that Mother urged me to try on hardtack didn't taste too bad. Smokey purred over a saucer of warm milk.

That night the storm struck our cabin. It was good we had milk and chocolate as we remained indoors except for emergencies during the next three days. A new and angrier gale came roaring down through the trees to rattle the window and shake the cabin. We stuffed the last of the papers in the cracks between the floor and wall. Gusts of wind sent the smoke back into the room. That sagey smell of burning brush mingled with the odors of the potty, for we couldn't get to the outhouse. Every day we looked for Dad's return and now as I watched Mother's frown deepen, my worries kept pace.

When Mom ventured out to tend Minniehaha or empty the potty, she had to shovel a path from the door for the snow had piled up as high as the latch. From the doorway she looked like a dark shadow moving out there in the murky haze of blowing snow.

On the first day of the big storm we ran out of kerosene for the lamps and oil burner. On the third day the wood pile was empty.

Mother said we would go to bed and tell stories. She tried to make it sound like fun, but something in her eyes and voice told me she was frightened. Were we going to die? I thought of the frozen birds and rabbits we usually kept in our snow cupboard and wondered if it hurt to freeze before you died.

But when I woke up in the morning it seemed the whole world was frozen—it was that quiet.

And then, suddenly there was a shout. "Tess! Turk, you okay?"

Mother and I raced to the front door and there was the old buckboard coming up the road with Dad leaning out trying to see us. What a happy moment that was!

"Daddy!" I shouted, running to meet him.

His face was white with worry. He seemed as relieved to find us safe as we were to see him. That night we celebrated. The relief and feast of words were even better than hot chili beans and canned peas with thick slices of bread. Best of all my parents appeared glad to see each other. There was no quarreling. Dad had brought magazines and newspapers. Mother was so happy that her cheeks grew extra pink and her small, deeply set hazel eyes held flecks of gold dust. I thought how pretty she was—how dear to me. Silently I vowed that when I grew up I would take care of her and make her this happy always.

Dad told us that the storm had prevented even the arrival of the mud wagon from Elko. While the grade to The Divide remained closed he had spent the time with his friends, the Primeauxs.

We were lucky, he said, that the road had only been closed a little over a week. It would be another week, at least, before the grade to the mining camp at Jarbidge could open. There was serious concern about the folks at Jarbidge and a trail had been cut down Jack Creek.

"Food and mail are being taken in by snowshoe and horse-back," he said.

I felt lucky and happy to have Dad home and to have the cabin warm, filled with smells of food cooking again, and the wooden table cluttered with papers—news of a far away world.

Dad said that Woodrow Wilson had signed a declaration of war.

My father, the pacifist, was raving. "You wouldn't believe all the foofara in Tuscarora. Flags sticking out windows. A band playing in the church. Beats me how men can celebrate the prospects of killing one another."

Killing one another? I looked at the rifles on the splintered wall and remembered the blast of the gun the day Ben Robinson shot my squirrel. I remembered Dad killing the deer and felt the burn of terror in my throat. But when I thought of guns aimed at my parents or me, my stomach hurt and I turned my eyes from the wall.

"Why can't we stay here where we're safe?" I asked.

"Safe—?" My mother repeated with a questioning lift of her brows.

She looked at my father for a moment, then they broke into laughter. It was many years before I understood what had amused them.

Words

THE DAY WHEN I first connected phonetic sounds with the meaning of words, sparklers were lit in my mind that have never gone out. During that snow-bound winter, Mom and Dad were trying to teach me to read. Dad promised if I sounded out each syllable, the sounds would merge into meaning and the stories in *St. Nicholas Magazine* would talk to me. But although I spent hours sounding syllables, each page remained a jumble of phonetics. Nothing ever came together.

It was the same with my family. In the stories they read to me, usually there were a mother and dad and two or more children, talking and laughing together. Because of the weather, the three of us were squeezed together like a senseless scramble of letters on a page. As the wind whistled through the sage and rattled the tin on our roof, sounds inside became increasingly cross. The words were usually the same ones.

"You will never make any money digging in the dirt!" Mother cried. "Give up this crazy idea of making a fortune in those damn mines. Quit dreaming, Elmer Pedlar! Get a steady job and take responsibility for your family!"

And Dad would reply, "Can't you understand I've got a lot of labor invested in this mountain? We're going to make a strike any day. Soon I'll be able to give you and the Little Turk anything you want. I'd be a fool to give it all up now."

"I was the fool for having married you."

Then I would close my ears. At such times when I stood at the window gazing at the white mountains and frosted sage, I wished I could be alone to play imagination games. I longed to shut out my parents' voices. Not that they shouted; what filled the cabin was a constant drone of discontent hovering like a threat. I watched the wind pick up a coffee can or piece of kindling and carry it across the endless stretch of snow. It was this sense of bountiful space that I loved most about my home and I couldn't understand why Mother would want to leave here.

But Mom talked constantly about California.

Sometimes Dad walked out on a quarrel. But he couldn't get far unless he went to Tuscarora. On days when he planned this trip, he sang while he shaved. I can see him standing in front of the small, round mirror in the kitchen, soaping a three- or four-day beard with the lathered shaving brush. Then he contorted his facial muscles while drawing the razor toward his chin before washing in the basin of soapy water on the shelf below the mirror.

Sometimes he would sit on the scarred kitchen stool while Mother cut his hair. A thick mop of curly brown hair covering his large head was beginning to gray and to recede from his naturally high forehead. A big nose failed to dominate his features. Sensitive lips, a barometer of his emotions, were quick to smile at adversity. Light blue eyes looked out on the world with a mixture of empathy and humor.

During that early spring it was Mother's actions that worried me most. I'd catch her unwrapping the fancy dresses that my California aunts sent from City Of Paris on my birthdays and at Christmas. She appeared occupied sorting out clothes and sewing on buttons. Often she started a conversation with the words, "When we get back to California . . ."

If I thought about leaving I'd get a stomach ache.

One morning I heard Dad singing while he shaved and I guessed he was going to town. I hoped he'd take me along.

Oh Wally, Wally, Wally wake me
Before it gets too late . . .

This was the place in the song where I'd learned to act straight man and I chirped, "Where yuh goin', Mo?"

Goin' ta swing on the Gold-en Gate . . .

He never sang as loud or sounded as free while he was shaving in the cabin as he did driving the buckboard to Tuscarora. I enjoyed Dad's baritone against the background clatter of horses' hooves and the rattle and squeak of the old buckboard that morning. The familiar smell of early summer heat, of dust and sage, greeted us while we bounced happily over the ruts in the mountain road. Behind us the buckboard carried ore and we made the first stop at Dexter's Mill. Outside the mill, a group of five men shoveled sage brush, a good and inexpensive fuel, into the feed hopper. Some of the men called out, "Hello, Ped." He climbed down from the buckboard and talked to them while they unloaded. Usually the talk was about weather. That day it would be about the heavy winter and the disasters of washouts to mills and mines while both the Carson and Bull Run rivers raged. Weather, it seemed, was never right for miners. A dry year meant a poor one, as the creeks and rivers failed to supply the necessary water for hydraulic mining, the cheapest method of working placer mines.

Yet a winter of heavy storms, such as the one that had held us snowbound, could wipe a miner out. Fortunately our mines were not near a river, only a stream. With the creek racing, Dad guessed it would be a rewarding year.

So on that day, dreams in his blue eyes glistened like fine gold in the rocks while he took me inside to explain how the mill worked. The mechanical process in those days before the gasoline engine involved shoveling the ore into a machine for fine grinding. Then the moistened pulp, mixed with quicksilver and a little salt, was placed in a circular enclosure and trampled by horses and mules. Fascinated, yet disturbed, I watched the dusty animals go around and around. What, I wondered, did they think about people who made them take so many steps without going any place? Horses did just about anything men wanted them to do and it seemed no one ever remembered to thank them.

Then Dad called to me to explain how an amalgam was being formed beneath the animals feet. I probably nodded because he had explained this word when we were "panning" and he'd showed me how the quicksilver snatches up the gold in the pan.

"An amalgam," he said, "is a blend of different things in the same way as a cookie is."

I knew when Dad picked up gold, either in the form of nuggets or liquid, it would be shipped by wagon train to Elko, then train to San Francisco. There, I learned later, it was evaluated at the assayer's office according to current market price.

Dad took considerable gold out of his Nevada mines, but by the time the mill costs, plus transportation and assayer, were paid, we barely eked out a living.

That day, after the ore had been unloaded, we drove into town where we left the horses and wagon at the stable. I paused to pat Dolly and Jerky on their noses and to thank them for the ride. Dad seemed to like that idea for he thanked them, too, and after that we never forgot again.

We walked down the main street of Tuscarora, called Weed Street after Bill Weed, one of the founders, who had filed claim to the famous DeFrees Mine. Three short streets, Front, Main, and West, crossed Weed Street. Whether it was on this trip or a future one, I remember passing the Cabinet Saloon, on the corner of Weed and Main, where the pungent smell of cigar smoke mingled with liquor drifted out in a blue stream above swinging doors. On we walked past a two-story framed building with a peaked roof for shedding snow. The lower floor housed Roach's Restaurant. Most all roofs in town were made from material at hand such as gallon cans, opened and hammered flat.

It was likely that we stopped at the firehouse for Dad to exchange a few words with the boys, who always welcomed him warmly. Hand in hand we strolled, our feet drumming a pleasant hollow thump on the wooden sidewalks patched with snow. Two public outhouses, roofs sagging, stood in knee-high weeds.

Dad was sure to point down Front Street with the fascinating information that the Chinese resided in that section. I recall those buildings trimmed with red and green paint: incense drifted from the Joss House and clothes waved from multiple lines behind the Wash House. The Chinese, Dad explained, were descendants of railroad builders, many of whom settled here as squatters after being driven from San Francisco. One of Dad's friends, a Mr. Hi Li, ran a laundry. Most of the Chinese were miners, but all grew their own vegetables and some opened stores to sell produce.

Was it that day we stopped at a small Chinese restaurant, The Gem? Quong was proprietor, chief cook, head waiter, and kitchen flunkey. Dad had heard that Quong made the best pies from dried peaches and apricots. We always sat at the counter and ate the most delicious sugar doughnuts I'd ever tasted. Maybe the unfamiliar smells in The Gem added to my enjoyment. The strange food tasted the way oriental incense smelled. No doubt I was licking sugar off my lips when Dad showed me the edge of town where the Indians lived in tents and huts. They were available, he said, for cheap domestic help. I thought of Mother carrying the heavy buckets of water from the creek and wished she could afford help.

This walk would take us by many saloons—the Idaho Saloon, Delta Saloon, Brewery Saloon, and Tuscarora Saloon before we arrived at the Town Tavern run by another friend, Buck Horn, who owned the saloon at The Divide. Buck Horn, a lanky, young man with a tough exterior and a special smile for me, always greeted Dad heartily. Dad was never without stories to share. From the men in the bar he would receive immediate attention.

"What's new, Ped? Say, tell us about that time in Mexico . . ."

Many times I'd perched on that high bar stool to drink lemonade while Dad told about amusing incidents that had occurred during his travels. One man asked Dad to recite "The Ballad of Pious Pete." Another wanted "Dangerous Dan McGrew."

Buck Horn asked me what poem I liked best. My answer was always the same. "Spell of the Yukon." It was about gold and my father.

I can see Dad standing in the saloon, his face shadowed by kerosene lanterns, facing the bar stools. He would gesture with both hands, maimed fingers tucked under. I can hear his pleasing baritone rolling out the words, bringing the poet's feelings to life:

> *I wanted the gold and I sought it;*
> *I scrambled and mucked like a slave.*
> *Was it famine or scurvy, I fought it;*
> *I hurled my youth into a grave.*
> *I wanted the gold and I got it—*
> *Came out with a fortune last fall,*
> *Yet somehow life's not what I thought it,*
> *And somehow the gold isn't all.*

On and on he went describing the summer in the mountains; for me he was describing our home.

> *There's a land where the mountains are nameless . . .*

All the poems that were in his head always amazed me.

> *. . . yet it isn't the gold that I'm wanting*
> *so much as just finding the gold.*
> *It's a great, big, broad land way up yonder,*
> *It's the forests where silence has lease.*
> *It's the beauty that fills me with wonder,*
> *It's the stillness that fills me with peace.*

I liked that poem because the poet talked about Dad and me. He put my feelings about the mountains into words.

Soon the men were laughing, drinking mugs of beer while they talked of the big storm, hopes for a big year at The Divide, politics, and the big question of war in Europe.

Sooner or later Buck Horn would reprimand someone for bad language.

"Watch your words, Red. There's a young one here."

When we left, I asked Dad what made words bad.

Words, he explained, were only sounds for communication.

"So-called bad words, Little Turk, change from generation to generation. After while the shock value wears out so new words appear."

He explained blasphemy and went on to say that all the bad words, when he was young, were about religion. But after repetition, words like "hell" or "damn" lost shock value. Now what he termed "out-house words" were in use and he wondered what would follow after all the shock words had been used and discarded.

"People," he said, "use bad words in the same way as babies scream when they need attention."

I began to understand that it was the thoughts behind words that made them good or bad. After that whenever I heard men swearing in a bar, I remembered they were crying like babies needing attention—and I felt sorry for them.

Our next stop on the splintery sidewalk would be the Primeaux Store. I remember Dad's eagerness for me to meet the two Primeaux boys. I was nervous.

Roy Primeaux and Dad were special friends. Roy, an educated man with a French accent, had a quick sense of humor. Both men enjoyed discussing politics.

My memory of this first meeting with Antoine Primeaux, whose path was destined to cross mine in surprising ways, is vague. But I can still see him clearly, a sturdy boy with red cheeks, fair hair, and a twinkle of mischief in brown eyes. He was close to my age. I must have stole curious glances at him that day as I had not seen any children for a long time. Besides, embarrassed at being so shy, I was ashamed of my stupid silence.

Antoine's younger brother, Pat, had darker skin, black hair, and no time for girls.

Antoine showed me the store. I was fascinated. I retained the impression of a huge store in the way that everything is magnified for a child. It was well stocked with mining equipment, supplies for the hunter and fisherman, sewing machines, pots, pans, and other hardware. But it was the shelves of toys that I liked best: trains, wagons skis, skates, dolls, books, and . . . especially, one small red sled.

I was longingly gazing at that sled, when Antoine's mom called to him to take the family wash on his wagon to the Chinese Wash House.

After we'd said goodbye, I wondered if Mom could take our wash to the Wash House instead of doing it in the river, if we might become a family like Antoine's.

We crossed town to the Butcher Shop near the stock yards, and I got the first whiff of that worst of odors and held my nose. But while the smell was repugnant, it was the mooing and bleating of animals that made those moments the worst in the day. They sounded so mournful and frightened I was certain they must know about the slaughter.

We returned to the post office, two doors from the Primeauxs, then made our final stop at Mrs. Rose's Grocery and Dry Goods Store. Here we would load the wagon with basic supplies: potatoes, rice, beans, canned food, and the hardtack, which the locals called Camp Cookies.

In front of Mrs. Rose's store that day I made a startling discovery. Attracted by a colorful advertisement in the fly-spotted window, I asked Dad what it said.

"Sound it out," he suggested. "What's the first syllable?"

I studied the word in bold black print.

"Cho—?"

"Chaw—" he nodded encouragement as he tied the reins to the hitching post.

"Chaw-co-late?" I asked, pressing my hands against the window front.

"Lat," he corrected. "Now try it again."

I repeated the senseless syllables slowly. Then my eyes found the familiar Ghirardelli can in the picture.

"Chocolate!" I squealed, and looked at my father. I think I knew Edison's feeling when his globe lit up.

Something Scary Out There

THEY WERE QUARRELING AGAIN. I wanted to whisper as I usually did, "Close ears so can't hear." But something awful was going to happen and I had to know.

"Elmer," Mother said in her scolding voice, "Do you realize Shirley will soon be eight years old?"

I was three months past seven that June of 1917, but when Mother had a point she refused to let truth get in her way. She reminded Dad that I needed to be in school. "You can't keep her buried in the wilderness forever." Did he, she would ask, want his child to grow up ignorant?

"The Turk reads and writes better now than most kids do at eight or nine," Dad would reply. Even when he was serious his voice often held some leftover laughter.

Mom would say something like: "To listen to you, Elmer Pedlar, you'd think books and reading were the only things a child learns in school."

"I would say she's gained some insight of the kind schools don't teach," Dad might reply, "and we haven't neglected math."

"You mean I haven't neglected it, don't you?"

"I give you full credit, Tereda." With a half bow and teasing smile, Dad would make his sweeping gesture with both hands bestowing that credit. "I've been reviewing multiplication tables on each trip to the outhouse."

Mom would persist that there were some things that neither she nor Dad could teach me, such as how to behave with other children. "Sometimes I think she believes she's a doe or a chipmunk—" Then with a startled glance at me, she would break off. "Run along and play, darling. Take your rod and catch a fish."

They were silent as I obediently reached for my fishing rod hanging on the cabin wall. But I was barely outside when I heard Mother say:

"I'm going to leave you, Elmer. I want to take Shirley home to California. I have to have money."

"If I had any, Tereda, you'd be welcome." Dad replied. "Maybe by next spring—"

According to Lydia Pinkham's calendar that hung on the wall, this was June 1917. When was spring? I was frightened.

"You can't stall me any longer. I'm returning to California if we have to walk!"

California. What was it really like? Having been only five when we left, my memories were misty. We must have been living with Mother's sister on the peach ranch in Selma for some time, for I could remember nothing previous to that ranch. There were cats, a dog, and a creaky windmill. It seemed that the ranch house was huge and that my aunt and uncle laughed a lot. I believe now that my parents must have been separated at that time.

Mother talked about fine restaurants and stage shows in San Francisco and family parties. Dad told different stories.

He said Mom forgot about the racket in the city. He described labor problems and crime. "Bombing by the unions," he would say, "and looting and the stink of manure in the streets."

It sounded awful.

But Mother always disagreed. She would remind him that we had been stuck "in this God-forsaken place" for two years. Things had changed, she said. Her sister, Kitty, wrote that she and Will had a new car. "None of my sisters drive buggies anymore."

Dad would make his usual remark about never winning an argument with her. Then the heavy silence would return.

Dad's three mines on Independent Mountain bore his pet names for Mother, her sister Agnes, and me—The Tereda, the Aganini, and the Turk Quartz. Somewhere in the background of our lives, the mines that Dad laid claim to also laid claim to us. For Mother, they were fetters. For Dad, dreams resided in these dark, mountain caverns, dreams of a day when he would strike a rich vein. Yet if he became a millionaire, I had little doubt he would choose to live in a mountain cabin with a stack of books and a mountain stream full of trout. It was clear that the gamble of the adventure was more important to him than the gold.

For me, the mines provided a wonderful game. Dad was teaching me to pan for gold. He brought a jug filled with quicksilver down to the river's edge. After warning me that quicksilver was poisonous and I should be careful to touch it only with the end of my long iron rod and not to breathe the fumes, Dad gave me my first lesson. When I think about it, I can hear his words:

"There's an art to panning, Turk, like flipping pancakes."

"Are we going to flip the mercury?"

"No, we're not ready for mercury yet." Then he would explain how I was to hold the pan full of gravel. I learned to immerse it in the quiet part of the stream enough to cover the pan and its contents.

"Like this?" I would ask.

"That's it." He would warn me that I must be especially careful for the next operation. While one hand held the pan, the other hand stirred the gravel, breaking up lumps. "Careful now—don't lose any."

Dad used a small rubber paddle but, as we had only one, I used a stick.

If any clay was in the pan it "must be puddled" until it was all dissolved. When the water became muddy it was time to dip the pan into the river. "See why we need to be by the creek?"

Dad helped me freshen the water in my pan, and waited until most of the gravel was dissolved. Then he instructed me to toss out the big stones and pebbles.

"Now," he would say, "comes the difficult part. Always remember you can enjoy any job once you get the hang of performing to music."

"Music?" I must have given him a bewildered look. We didn't own a Victrola.

"We make our own." He explained that the sensation of body movement to music has mysterious effects on people, important in perfecting any skill: cooking, fishing—and panning.

"Watch this." I can see him grasp the pan, still under water, with both hands and move it in a circular motion. He accompanied himself with "Yankee Doodle." First one way—"Yan-kee, Doo-dle"—then—"went to to-wn"—. Now into reverse—"ri-din' on a po-ny . . ."

Fascinated I watched his graceful and adept movement as the contents of the pan moved from side to side. But when I tried I spilled the gravel every time. Patiently Dad refilled my pan and started me over. I kept asking if it was time for the mercury.

"Not yet. Like anything new this takes practice, Turk."

I watched as, after giving the heavy particles time to settle, he removed the pan from the stream. Then came the most difficult part for me.

He tilted his pan forward. "To about 12:15," he said, and showed me how the lighter sand washed over the lip of the pan. At the same time, Dad quickly dipped the top into the stream and out, while he continued to whistle.

"Here is where the drummer comes in." He picked up a block of wood and gave the pan a few vigorous blows on the bottom, singing "Boom, boom, boom. There." He said that helped settle the gold particles, then he let me do it.

We worked until Dad said it was time to wash the heavy sand and gold down with black sand, and put it out to dry. In the meantime we started panning more gravel.

I doubted I'd ever become as adept as my father. He made it look so easy. When Dad put a small amount of black sand and gold particles in my amalgamated copper-bottomed pan and ever so carefully sprinkled about a teaspoon full of the expensive silver mercury on the surface, I enjoyed this process most. I stirred the gold and sands with a piece of black iron, while I sang "Oh! Susannah." When the mercury contacted all the gold particles it formed what Dad called an amalgam, a word I'd heard recently while visiting Dexter's Mill. I started paying a lot of attention to words since Dad told me I'd need to store many of them away if I hoped to write stories someday.

Now it was surplus mercury that we tried to save in another dish, as it was expensive. That Dad trusted me to handle something so costly and poisonous added to my pleasure. He explained that the gold he panned was a sampling he took when it appeared he may have struck a rich vein. Subsequently the "color ore" was loaded in the buckboard and hauled down to Tuscarora to the mill.

Many times I'd questioned him about the blasting. Even from the cabin, at least a mile away, I shivered at the sound of the explosion of dynamite.

When we returned to the cabin for lunch, I begged to go with him and watch.

Dad hesitated.

"It's no place for a child," I can hear Mother say as she set a pot of fragrant baked beans on the table. Then she would tell me that it was very frightening, and might be dangerous. That day she planned to ride Dolly to the post office and asked if I didn't want to come with her.

I begged to go with Dad and see him blast.

Even Mother's offer to buy peppermint sticks at Buck Horn's Saloon and Post Office didn't tempt me.

Finally Dad said he'd take me if I promised to do exactly what he said. He would be too busy to keep an eye on me.

"No!" Mother must have broken in. "It's too dangerous."

It was always Mother who decided what I could or could not do. I guessed Dad was ready to give in.

"I'm not a baby," I would protest. "Can't I ever, ever see? I'll do exactly what you tell me—please, Dad?"

Mother said that no one knows what they'll do when they're frightened. "People panic sometimes, darling." She warned me that I couldn't imagine the noise until I was close to it, that dirt would get in my eyes. She promised that I wouldn't like it.

I brightened. When she talked like this she was going to give in.

And, after more arguments, she finally warned me again to be careful, adding that I'd be sorry I hadn't listened to her. As we went off, my hand in my father's, I had a delightful sensation, not of excitement alone but of highly intensified fear. Mother's words—"You don't know what you'll do when you become frightened"—challenged, rather than intimidated me. Since I didn't know, I had to find out. Would it be more scary than seeing the snake coming up through the floor after me? As scary as the sound of the gun when Dad killed the deer?

Dangerous, my parents said. Dad and I slowed our steps as we climbed the mountain approaching the mines, but my heart raced faster and faster. We passed the long construction that looked like a boarded-in slide. Dad said it was called a Long Tom. Then in words similar to these, he explained the process:

"It's a sluice box, Turk. Remember the process when we panned for gold? The Long Tom goes through about the same steps but it handles a lot more ore than the team of you and me."

At the lower end of the Long Tom, a piece of coarse screen was set, at what Dad would call "a quarter to one" degree angle, for the sand and fine gold to fall through. The screen prevented the coarse gravel from going to the riffle box, which was the second section.

Dad showed me where he had lined the riffle box with his old corduroy jacket plus a piece of canvas to catch the gold. I had seen Mom strain gold out of the tub after she washed his jacket.

He explained how the cross-riffles placed at the bottom caught the leaf gold and these, too, were removed for cleaning.

Sometimes I'd watched from below, when Dad and Huddleson were shoveling ore into the Long Tom. But I'd never seen the process up close until that day. The two men worked the gravel over with rakes to break up the clay.

I learned that sometimes mercury was used in the lower riffles to amalgamate the fine gold.

Dad paused on the side of the mountain and I knew we were within shouting distance of the mines.

"Listen carefully." He'd never sounded more serious than when he warned me that day to sit still and not get up.

When he shouted, "down" I was to lie flat and cover my ears. I was to stay like that until he told me that all was clear.

"W-where will you be?"

He explained that Hud was up at the mine. Dad was going to get the line and light the fuse. Then he'd be back with me before the dynamite went off.

It seemed that Dad was gone a long time and all of that time scariness kept growing.

Finally, he came down the mountain with the long cord. He lit the end of the fuse, tossed it, and after a moment dropped down on the grass beside me. Breathless, I watched the red glow snake up the mountain toward the Aganini Mine.

"Down!" he shouted. And then we were both on our stomachs, with his arm around my shoulders, his hand pressing my head down against the scratchy grass. Fear left his hand to travel up my neck to the hair roots.

We waited. Nothing happened. There was only the burning sun on my face and neck, the summer smell of earth, the buzz of insects. A waiting stillness threatened the air. An ant crawled up my arm.

"Suppose it's gone out, Ped?" Huddleson's shout rang down the mountain.

Dad cupped his hands and shouted through them. "I'm sure not going up to find out!"

A shudder raced along my spine. Then it came. The biggest noise I'd ever heard ringing in my ears. It boomed up out of the middle of the world. Beneath me, the earth shook. The whole mountain trembled, and caught in that tremble I knew why people panicked. Yet terror only increased curiosity. Cautiously I raised my head, straining to see while dirt stung my eyes. Rocks shot upward. Dust turned the air into a haze. Then rocks and boulders started down the mountain, crashing, leaping, flying. But Dad had situated us in a place out of danger from falling rocks. The unusual odor of the explosion and the smell of dust and heat became the smell of terror. If the earth could open up like this and pitch its own soil and rocks skyward, it was clear that it could no longer be trusted. Then . . . there was no place to be safe. Neither Dad nor Mom could protect me. I felt a prickle like gritty sand on my scalp. All the talk I'd recently heard of union bombings and of war in Germany with Huns dropping torpedoes came back in a rush. I asked Dad if torpedoes were like blasting and he nodded.

Somewhere, right now, the earth was blowing up like this. Somewhere people—buried alive! Or locked in submarines to drown on the bottom of the ocean. The tremor gripped me and went on and on until I discovered the earth was still, only my body shook. I clung to the sensation. Thinking about bombs and the war, I took refuge from fear by working that fear up to panic. Panic brought a peculiar pleasure. I let all the danger in the air close in around me: dreaded, even while I gloried in, threats from the sky and beneath my body—felt the danger through my pores, smelled it, heard it again and again. Never before had every part of me been so gloriously alive.

But the terror and wonder of that day were not yet over.

When Dad and I returned to the cabin, Mother was lying down in her petticoat. I knew at once something was wrong. She never rested in the daytime. The big wooden tub stood in the center of the floor and the room smelled of steam. Why hadn't she emptied her bath water?

Dad went instantly to her. "Tereda, what's wrong?"

That was when I noticed two things almost at the same time: a big blue bruise on Mother's arm and an ugly scratch on her neck.

I ran to climb up on the bed beside her. It was the second time in one day that I felt the earth tremble. I wanted to know what had hurt her.

She managed a shaky smile and told me she'd fallen off the horse.

I was amazed. Why would Mom fall off Dolly Grey? Dolly was gentle and obedient. Mom could ride well.

Dad urged her to tell us about it.

Instantly Mom glanced at me and I knew what that glance meant. This was something I was not to hear.

She said she was shook up and came home to bathe.

Then she broke off and I saw she was fighting tears.

Dad glanced up at the wall, then his voice sent out alarm. "Where's the rifle?"

She explained that it must have dropped off the saddle when she fell. But I caught her frowning at him and shaking her head. What was it that she didn't want me to know? Mom wasn't a dreamer like Dad and me. Even if she fell off the horse and was hurt, she'd remember the rifle. This just wasn't like my capable mother. I was puzzled.

I knew Dad was going to tell me to run along outside while he talked to Mother alone. He did.

"Why do I have to?" I asked Dad, who often gave in.

"Just do as you're told," Mother said. And when she spoke I went.

About a half hour later, Dad came out and went back to the stable to harness Dolly. When I asked where he was going, he told me he was going to look for the gun. I'd never seen his face so red and angry. Why had Mother's fall made him cross?

That night, I stayed awake long after the kerosene lamp was turned out. Outside I heard the pleasant hum of crickets, but after a time I heard the howl of wolves and felt the threat return from somewhere out there.

Now I knew that even when we were happy the threat was there—waiting. Mother wasn't afraid of anything and yet . . . Before I went to bed, I asked her if the blast made her fall off Dolly.

Shaking her head, she hugged me. Then she reminded me that when I was so frightened about the snake I didn't want to hear people talk about snakes? "I don't want to talk about what happened today."

These words scared me more than ever. If there were things from somewhere out there that could scare even Mother, what kind of things could they be?

A long time later when my parents must have thought I was asleep I heard their voices. This is what I remember of that conversation.

Dad said it was a good thing for old Brandy Crawford that Buck took him down to the doc before Dad got there. "If I'd seen him he'd have a lot more than a bullet in his foot . . ." He puzzled me by murmuring something about Mother being lucky.

"Luck has nothing to do with knowing how to shoot," Mother retorted, sounding cross. Then she said the strangest thing, "He's the lucky one. I didn't aim for his chest!"

Sitting up on my cot in the lean-to, I was baffled by what I heard. How had Brandy Crawford got the bullet in his foot? And why did my parents sound so mad at him? I missed something Dad said.

Then Mother's voice rose and she said she wasn't going to be buried in this forsaken hole any longer. I remember her saying, "A child grows peculiar in such an isolated place."

We were leaving The Divide! I found these words more scary than all the combined terror of that strange day. Leave The Divide . . . ? I wasn't sure what "peculiar" meant but I guessed it had something to do with The Wad. If I didn't do this bad thing, maybe we wouldn't be leaving.

Dad was silent for a time. Then he agreed that a change might not be a bad idea because winters here were tough on a woman. Then he added that they could be pretty tough on young men, too. "Seldom they see a woman . . ." He suggested we might go down to Tuscarora before the snow set in.

"Tuscarora!" Mother cried in disgust. "What am I supposed to do in that burg without money?"

Dad replied that he had friends "who would put you and the Turk up." I guessed he meant Antoine's parents.

Mother told him he had no pride. She would never accept charity. Her voice broke and I wondered if she were crying, but her next words sounded even more angry. She promised that she would find a way and when she did . . . we were never, never coming back.

"Never—never coming back." Those words kept fluttering in my chest like caged birds' beating wings.

"You can come with us, Elmer Pedlar or—you—you can go to—to the devil."

I would never forget her words because it was the first time I'd ever heard Mother say a bad word. I guessed she must be crying inside like a baby and I felt sad for her. Dad didn't answer. It was true then. We were going to leave him—leave our home.

I smothered sobs in my pillow. I couldn't imagine living anywhere except here. Would Mother really take me away from Dad and from all my animal friends and The Sandy Shore? I wondered if pretend people in your stories would come with you any place or did they stay behind? I was certain they would remain here.

When I woke before dawn, my imagination raced with possibilities of what had happened. Maybe Mother had seen a bear. That was silly. She wouldn't fall off her horse, she'd ride faster. Maybe Brandy Crawford had frightened Dolly Gray, causing her to fall. He scared me once when I saw him drunk in Buck Horn's saloon, but . . . it was all too puzzling.

I'd thought Mom wasn't afraid of anything. But it must have been something really bad that frightened her because she said it was like the snake—too awful to even think about. Mother said she didn't want to talk about it—ever. Would she change her mind someday and tell me?

She never did.

1917: Being Different

SHORTLY AFTER THE BLASTING, Dad prepared to drive to Tuscarora again. Mother announced that we would go with him. Not knowing what she had in mind, I was eager to go. I guessed we would see the Primeaux boys again and maybe stop at The Gem Restaurant for sugar doughnuts.

Mother suggested that Dad go on to Mrs. Rose's Grocery while she and I stopped by the post office.

I was mildly surprised that she didn't want to go and buy groceries because she'd always supervised Dad's purchases. He, an impulsive buyer, was inclined to choose bars of chocolate and canned fruit, which Mom declared extravagant. She would buy big packages of oatmeal, dried milk, rice, macaroni, and all that dull food.

While Mom went in the post office, I discovered a tabby cat with a litter of kittens underneath the wooden sidewalk. By stretching out on my side at the curb and reaching under the walk, I could feel those little live things! Baby kittens! The spunky kittens spat at me as my arm stretched into their hiding place. I didn't mind the scratches I received before pulling out a tri-colored kitten. Intent on begging Mother to let me keep it, I hurried into the post office.

Except for Mother and Dora La Marr, the small room was deserted. Dora had come around from behind the counter and the two young women stood closely together, talking in low voices.

Mother was saying she needed someplace for us to stay. Then

she told Dora she intended to look for a job and would never return "to that awful life."

I must have stood there, wordless. We weren't going home with Daddy! It had happened. The thing I most dreaded. I nearly dropped the kitten.

And then I said the first thing that came to mind. "Mother, we have to go home! I left Smokey there."

Both women whirled to look at me.

Dora, a pretty young woman with long, dark hair always spoke in a slow sad tone as if she were telling bad news. She may have remarked on my finding a new kitten, than asked how I would like to stay with her for a time.

I shook my head and explained that my dad would miss us. Besides there was Smokey, and my chipmunks and the robin and Haha and—I turned to Mother, begging her to take me home.

Mother said that Dad would take care of my pets. "It's time we get you in school."

School! A room filled with strange children. The thought terrified me. Besides I couldn't imagine living in Tuscarora. For a day's trip it could be fun but never, never could it be home. I kept thinking of Mom's words to Dora La Marr: "I have no intention of returning to that awful life ever!"

She couldn't really mean that, could she? I couldn't believe we wouldn't go home. What would Dad do? What would I do without animal friends, trees to climb, a stream to wade in, and a place alone to tell stories?

To console me, Mom let me keep the kitten. But pleasure in the calico cat had been snuffed out by worry. Daddy won't leave us here, I thought. I should have known better. Once my mother's mind was made up, Dad never stood a chance.

When Mom removed a bulging suitcase from the back of the buckboard, Dad looked startled.

"You're not coming home, Tereda?" He asked what she intended to do.

Mother replied she would get a job and look after herself and me.

I can hear Dad say what he always said, "I haven't much money to leave you," he said.

And Mom's reply would be the same as it always was, "I didn't expect you would. You never will."

I clung to him and sobbed that I wanted to go home.

Mom put an arm around me but I shrugged her off. She promised that Dad would be coming to see us soon.

He hugged me, then knelt down to explain. It was better that I stay with my mother and start school.

"If you want to write your stories someday, you'll need to learn a few things at the little schoolhouse, Turk." He promised to take good care of Smokey and my small farm. Then he said he'd be back with Smokey in less than a month.

That seemed like a very long time. We stayed the night with Dora La Marr. I'd been put to bed in an upstairs room. It was an empty shell of a house and it felt hollow. Maybe it was me that felt hollow; I couldn't be sure. But the bare floor squeaked and thumped like a drum beneath my feet. The stairs were crooked and barely wide enough for a child's feet. The bedroom had a slanted ceiling so I could only stand up straight on one side of the room. Mom and Dora had to bend over when they came up. Dora was poor because she didn't have much furniture, I guessed. That was when I first realized we were poor—even more than Dora for we no longer had a home.

The calico kitten cried most of the night and I made it a duet. I wondered if we'd ever return to our cabin. I knew Mother hated The Divide. If we weren't going back ever I wish someone had told me so I could have said a proper goodbye to everything: to The Sandy Shore and the trees, even to the old mean hawk who stole the robin's eggs. The thought of days ahead without my Dad filled the dark, and the hollow place inside widened and widened. I missed the sound of Smokey purring in the dark room and the warmth of his body on my feet. I made a wish with my eyes squeezed shut that Mother wouldn't find a job so we'd have to go home.

I thought of Dad returning to the deserted cabin with no dinner cooking. And of Smokey, who would be scared because I'd disappeared. I thought of the window behind the table that looked out on sage and chipmunks, birds, squirrels, rabbits, and an occasional possum. I remembered the friendly mountain stars that came close to my window.

Dora La Marr's house had running water and a stove twice the size of our tiny one. There were five rooms, one attic bedroom up a rickety staircase, and only sparse furnishings. Although the faded wallpaper was peeled in a few places, the house was okay except, for me, any house in Tuscarora would be awfully lonely. Outside, a tar-paper roof and flattened tin from the kerosene cans provided weather proofing, the same as on our cabin.

A stereoscope, which had belonged to Dora's mother, fascinated me more than any object in that house. For long periods of time I amused myself by fitting two pictures into the rack about two feet from my nose, then looking through the double eye glasses as the scenes magically blended into one.

But whenever possible I sneaked upstairs and tried to escape depression in a story. It was difficult because I still found The Wad, as a vehicle, more effective than a pencil. Sitting in the middle of the bed with a corner of the blanket squeezed between intense fingers I was distracted by fear of Mother and Dora La Marr walking in on me. And that was exactly what happened.

On a day when the frantic bobbing of The Wad failed to release my muse, I squirmed on the bed, frustrated as a race horse tied at the post. Then I heard voices but before I could release The Wad, Mother and Dora La Marr stood in the doorway.

"What are you doing?" Mother asked sharply. I believe she was so startled to catch me at the imagination game she despised, that momentarily she forgot her resolution to ignore the situation.

Then she covered up quickly, suggesting I was tired of being inside and that we should all go for a walk. I must have agreed, relieved at not being forced to explain.

Outside boot prints and sled tracks marked a path in the slushy snow for us leading to Weed Street. Each winter, Mr. Primeaux, who owned a Maxwell, and two other men in town who owned cars drove the vehicles back and forth on a few of the town streets to make a road to the schoolhouse. Now, in June, snow was melting and large patches of ground were visible.

Dora La Marr and my mother were near the same age, a little past thirty. It had been a long time since Mother had a woman friend. They sat up late at night, talking.

From the bed that felt too large and empty, I strained to eavesdrop. Bits of conversation reached me. No laughter. Once I thought I heard Mother sob. But maybe not, because her next words came in a clear commanding voice I knew well. "I've got to find a job, Dora. I don't know where. But I'm determined to get my child in school."

She won't find a job, I thought. She mustn't. Then we'll get to go back to Dad. But at times I faltered, noticing the twin frown lines deepening on her forehead or the sad look in her deeply set, hazel eyes. I guessed she was thinking about her dream of a pretty house in California. But I knew Dad would be unhappy anyplace except the mountains—same as I would. There seemed to be no way we could all be happy and together.

When I thought about school I considered running away. I thought I could find my way over Mt. Blitzen and back to the cabin. But Mother would only come after me. Being a child was a lot like being a cat. People could pick you up and take you wherever they pleased. Or they could go away and leave you as I'd left Smokey . . . as Dad had left me.

Then, I heard Dora La Marr's mournful voice from downstairs reporting there were only a few weeks left of the spring term. She suggested that Mother take me to school on Monday and ask the teacher, Miss Plum, what grade I might fit into.

Monday? But this was Friday. Dread rose in my throat. The only child I'd met was Antoine and I didn't know him well. A whole roomful of strange children was far more threatening than a forest of wild animals. I prayed to God and teased Mother not to send me.

If I waited any longer, she told me, I'd be a big girl in a kindergarten with a class of babies.

She might get a job, she explained, so we could stay here in Tuscarora for a time before we returned to California. Dora La Marr thought a cook was needed at the local boarding house.

She asked Mother if she had ever cooked for a gang of hungry men. "Do you think you can do it, Tess?"

Mother retorted that she had grown up cooking for crews on a sheep ranch. "I can do anything I have to."

On Monday morning Mother brought out the blue wool jumper with a white dimity blouse, ruffled around the neck. It was one of the outfits sent by my Aunt Ann Williford, an outfit from San Francisco's elegant store City Of Paris. My California aunts always sent elegantly dressed dolls with china faces—too good to play with—and ruffled dresses too fancy to wear.

Mother combed my curly chestnut hair and it bobbed up in ducktails and curls. She looked pleased with the way I looked and happier than she'd appeared for a long time. I studied the stranger in Dora's cracked mirror and my anxiety grew. Did everyone dress up so fancy for school? Mother assured me that no one would look better.

First we went with Miss La Marr to the post office. I stood outside on the wooden sidewalk waiting for Mother. A grubby boy came along. He took one look at me, then toppled down on the ground and began to eat dirt.

When I asked Miss La Marr what made him do that, she laughed. "Tommy has never seen a girl all dressed up—like a princess. He thought he'd seen a vision."

I panicked. "Doesn't everyone dress up for school?"

She hesitated. Then she explained that children here didn't have stylish city clothes like mine.

Before I could beg Mother to let me change, the terrifying gong-gong of the bell rang out from the small steeple over the schoolhouse. That bell was a sound I'd never forget. Mother hurried me across town to the small gray schoolhouse. Most of the desks—twenty I learned later—were occupied and from behind them, startled eyes focused on me. My cheeks flamed while I observed faded and worn clothing. How ridiculous I must look to them! Why hadn't Mother found out what I should wear? Oh, how I wished the elegant jumper had pockets to hide my nervous hands.

Miss Plum was young as my mother. She was pretty in a lively way. Coils of heavy brown hair circled her rather small head, and her watchful eyes were gentle. Mother held a whispered conference with Miss Plum, then bent and kissed me goodbye. Several kids snickered. Never had I held my mother with less regard. I shifted weight, hoping for a seat in the rear—soon.

Miss Plum pointed to a front seat, suggesting I sit there until she could test where I belonged.

I nodded. Something had happened to my voice. Had she seated me with the kindergarten? I was the tallest in the row! I tried to concentrate on the novelty of an ink well.

Big boys came in first; some must have been sixteen or seventeen. They sat on the opposite side of the room. Later I learned fifteen to eighteen pupils attended, depending on the weather. I was glad to see Antoine Primeaux's familiar face but I was too shy and miserable to return his smile.

All the faces in that school were white. Children from the Chinese section of town had their own school in the Buddhist Church. Indian children did not attend school. I never knew why.

"This is Shirley Pedlar, class," Miss Plum announced, adding that I would be a guest until she could find where I belonged. "Open your study books."

Smothered giggles broke into the silence. They were laughing at me. Then Miss Plum did something odd. She took me around the room and asked me to read the blackboards. She used a stick to point out two words written on each board—*I see*.

"I see," I whispered, for my voice had not returned. Then, again and again I recognized the two words as we circled the room and Miss Plum's pointer tapped the blackboard. "I see. I see. I see."

All my life when someone nods in conversation and murmurs, "I see," I'm back in that one-room schoolhouse confirming my understanding of those two words. What I understood was that school was worse than I'd ever imagined possible, a place where I first discovered I was different from my classmates. I didn't belong. I sensed it was more than my clothes.

Miss Plum praised me so heartily I was puzzled and felt compelled to whisper, "I can read."

When she asked what books I read, I replied in a whisper, "Dangerous Dan McGrew."

She looked startled then gave me some simple arithmetic. When I had completed the addition that I remembered from the walls of the outhouse, she moved me over two rows to the second grade.

Much later when I dared to study the room, I found I could pick members of the same family by patches; the calico patch on the jeans or the denim band to lengthen a skirt. Soon the first surprise of my classmates at my appearance turned to animosity. Children, safe and smug in conformity, banded together as if by instinct. Disgraced, I avoided their eyes. And I fidgeted. It was punishment to sit with fingers folded on the small desk for hours while I longed to be free to splash in the river or to scramble up the branches of a tree. All day I looked at the wall clock and each time the hands jerked through a minute I drew a heavy sigh. Finally the bell rang, but if anything could be worse than that schoolroom it was recess. Children gathered around me to stare.

One sandy-haired girl with freckles asked, "Why d'ya wear that party dress to school? Yuh look silly."

"I dunno," I muttered. I did know. Except for my City of Paris outfit, I had no clothes that fit me. In the mountains I wore dresses bursting at the seams or an outfit stitched by Mom out of one of her dresses. Mom's talent with the needle being limited, her stitches were about as reliable as a tent without stakes. But oh, how I envied the safety of those worn hand-me-downs! I must convince Mother that I couldn't possibly come back here tomorrow.

But when Mother met me at three o'clock, she announced proudly that she had a job cooking in the boarding house. With many young men having enlisted for the war, jobs for women were plentiful. Mom said that we would only be there a short time until she saved the fare to take us to California. Then everything would be wonderful.

I cried. I pleaded. I stamped my foot and rebelled. But I knew it was useless. When Mom made up her mind she was as stubborn as Haha.

"Darling," she said, as she had told me before, "I want you to have an education, all the things I never had." She told me how she used to visit art galleries and attend music concerts when she was pregnant with me. "I hoped you'd appreciate beautiful things."

The boarding house, near the school, could hardly be classed among "beautiful things." Our room adjoined the kitchen. Mother would receive room, board, and a small salary. That night she was making a rabbit stew. She had dug up onion bulbs from the yard and I watched her pull the yellow bulbs apart from the cluster. I used to wonder if this separation process was painful for onions.

In the morning, Mom was up at five to build a fire in the iron stove, to bake bread, and to start breakfast for seven boarders.

I shook out the ragged, grey calico dress I'd worn down in the buckboard. Calico, a coarse cotton, was a cheap fabric.

"You can't wear that." Mother sounded horrified. She reminded me that the dress was a mass of wrinkles and she didn't have time to iron it. She looked at my tearful face with apparent distress.

"Besides you've outgrown it. Oh darling, you look so pretty in that velvet jumper—"

"Nobody dresses like that."

When I started to sob, she gave in and took time to iron the calico. I went off to school, fittingly shabby. Yet the others continued to stare at me. I knew I'd never be accepted. I didn't belong. Antoine was my only friend and, at school, he played with boys.

I didn't dare ask Mom for a cotton dress because she was saving every penny for our fare to California. Dear Dora La Marr bought a piece of white calico from Mrs. Rose's General Store and made a middy school dress for me. Recently I came across a picture in that dress with Buck Horn and the two Primeaux boys. The short skirt starting below the hipline was outdated enough to conform to Tuscarora fashions. In the picture my underslip is hanging down, so clothes-wise I conformed fairly well. The deceiving "rich-girl-look" was gone forever. When Mrs. Rose had a sale Mother stitched up another "Tuscarora dress." But the harm was done. My classmates knew I was different. My only consolation was that school would soon be out. I counted days.

⁓

These things I remember: the big table in the boarding house where Mother served lunch and dinner, mostly to men; the smells of hearty stews, or mutton, venison or jack rabbit hash, baked beans, and home-made bread that permeated the house. There were pies: apple, wild berry, mincemeat, and pumpkin. A small, wizened Indian woman became a familiar sight behind the big stove. Her name may have been Minnie, which she pronounced "Meanie" in a voice that sounded like Calico's mewing. She carried her china bowl and begged for a portion of whatever was cooking. Mother filled the bowl. Later Meanie made an ineffectual effort to help by dabbing at the stove or dishes with her wet dish rag before returning to her place behind the stove.

Usually I had supper early and was in our room, sometimes studying, often escaping in an imagination game. After dinner, when the table was cleared, the men played poker.

They talked about gold strikes, told stories of miners made rich over night. And they argued about problems and the expense of freighting ore down to the mills. What caught my attention was the scary talk that the war with Germany was spreading.

Late that night, I asked Mother, "Is the war coming to Tuscarora?"

She tried to reassure me but I was no longer certain I could believe her. I began to catch her keeping things from me. What would happen when the Huns came roaring and shooting up the road from Elko?

If only Dad with Smokey would come in time to save us.

On sunny June days with the snow melting, children were warned to watch out for old mine shafts in the streets. Many were boarded over. But the boards were rotted and the shafts were deep and dangerous. Once a dog had fallen in and was never seen again. I couldn't bear to think about that dog.

The two weeks passed and school was finally out for summer.

On the Fourth of July flags were everywhere. And a surplus of orators expounded at the picnic. America had been in the war three months and a subject of increasing interest sprang from a recent editorial in the Elko *Daily Free Press*. According to a letter Mom wrote to her sister Agnes, this editorial claimed it was America's duty to "organize and assemble China, Russia, and America's armies so the three great Democracies can join hands around the world."

Many arguments started over whether or not Russia was a Democracy. "Breaking away from the Czar doesn't make it Democratic," Buck Horn would insist.

"It's Bolshevik, that's what it's becoming," Pastor Hawkins was likely to reply.

I asked Mom what a Bolshevik was. She said it meant a Russian who had different ideas about government from ours.

Following the speeches Barney Horn, Buck's brother, took up a collection "to buy smokes for our boys over there." Then there were horse and foot races, bronco busting, and some patriotic music by the school band. The older men played horseshoes while children lined up to jump rope. I was too shy to join in.

I helped Mom and the other ladies, who kept busy setting the long wooden tables with box lunches, filling pitchers of lemonade from milk buckets, or slicing homemade cakes.

I remember Mom talking about this particular picnic. There was a discussion, she later told her sisters, over a newspaper item she'd saved to share with them. It concerned President Wilson's remarks to the suffragists who demonstrated in Washington. "Good ladies," President Wilson had greeted them,

> *Why all the rudeness? Of what avail this bombast?*
> *Of what combination of gray matter is that which leads*
> *gentle bred women to violate all conventional rules of*
> *polite assemblages? To overlook the necessity of poise*
> *and dignity?*

The majority of women in Tuscarora probably agreed with President Wilson; some nodded their heads as they knitted socks for "our boys over there."

Knowing Mother I have no doubts as to what she retorted: "Sure, women should keep their mouths shut and work twelve hours a day for half a man's salary."

Whatever she said her remark brought silence and women exchanged glances. If only she'd keep quiet, I thought. It was just one more thing to make us different from everyone else.

It was near the end of July when Dad arrived with Smokey in a box. Both Smokey and I were overjoyed to be together again. Then I saw that Dad had come in the buckboard with Haha tied up behind. They must have brought part of the old me because I shouted and turned cartwheels on the street in front of the boarding house until Mom warned me I was showing my pants. Then I noticed that all of our belongings appeared to be in the wagon.

Weren't we ever going home? At least Dad had come back to us! But after a few moments, I caught his expression. He looked as he did when a hopeful vein of gold suddenly ended. I took his hand and rubbed the smooth ends of the finger stumps. He admitted he was broke and could get no more credit. For a short time he stayed in the boarding house with us. He insisted that his mines were rich with gold, but he lacked the means to get it down the mountain and assayed.

Mother pleaded with him as she always did to take us back to California. But Dad was not ready to give up his dream. He vowed he would get a job and save up a stake so he could return to The Divide. I understood how he felt. It was what I wanted most.

Shortly after the first of August, Dad was hired by the Columbia Mine in Bull Run County. During the severe storms of the previous winter, a snow slide turned into an avalanche and repairs were needed on the tunnel. It was ironic that the storm, threatening our lives a few months earlier, provided work for Dad when he needed it most. At first Mother refused to leave her job and go with him, but after a case of scarlet fever took the life of the judge's young son, she became anxious to get me out of town.

Bull Run is ninety-two miles northwest of Elko, near the Idaho border. Early one morning—"to get a start on the heat of the day," Dad said—we pulled out of Tuscarora, passed the old cemetery with its crooked crosses, and with our one horse, Dolly, pulling the old buckboard, headed north. Haha plodded along in the dust cloud behind us.

Dad didn't sing or whistle this time. Mother appeared to treat him especially nice. Maybe she sympathized with him, knowing something about lost dreams.

I'm sure I wondered if Bull Run would be the same as The Divide. Would I feel surrounded with my own family again? Oh, how eager I must have been to get to the mountains where my exiled memories could find a home.

Bull Run

THE BULL RUN MINING DISTRICT was discovered in 1869 and probably derives its name from the Civil War battles of 1861 and 1862, although the order of naming remains undetermined. The old mining camp lies around eighty-nine miles north from Carlin on the east slope of the Bull Run Mountains or Centennial Range. This north-south extending range forms the eastern limit of the Valley of the Owyhee. Bull Run River runs through a canyon of the same name north of Deep Creek and empties into Bull Run Reservoir. In the Humboldt National Forest one of the peaks bears the name of Bull Run Peak.*

On the night we arrived at Bull Run, we camped out near the bank of Bull Run River. As usual on such events, Dad fixed dinner over the camp fire, and afterwards he washed up. Mom caught our supper in the river. Fishing was the one recreation she enjoyed in the mountains and the result at Bull Run delighted her. In a short time, a string of rainbow trout hung from the branches of a cottonwood along the river.

Dad put up a tent. Mother made up a bed on the ground inside.

But sometime in the night it started to rain. In a few minutes it came down with the fury of a mountain squall in mid-August.

Mother was furious. Dad laughed and I joined in. Not even the threat of a battle could snatch away the joy of this adventure. Thunder roared like the mechanical elephant in my story. Rain,

---

*Nevada Place Names, Helen S. Carlson. University of Nevada Press, Reno: 1974.

pounding down on the tent, sounded like hail on a tin roof. Then a sudden splash of large raindrops bounced off the canvas covering our bed. I felt the warm shape of Smokey curled beside me: Calico served as a foot warmer. The shock of cold water falling on my face and running down my neck seemed like the funniest thing that had ever happened and I joined Dad in whoops and whoops of laughter.

Mother, the practical one, demanded that Dad get the buggy robe and his raincoat. She ordered him to get out and cover the leaks before we all got pneumonia.

Some small demon in me enjoyed lining up with Dad against Mom. In the ever present mother-daughter rivalry, I was way out front. Mother was my security and as I moved away from security the night opened up to freedom, freedom more glorious for being tinged with fear. Out there in the dark forest lurked the unknown. Out there a fierce wind lashed the trees where danger hid. Yet the mountain wind carried a smell of the wild, a reminder that we breathed the same air with one another—and with our mountain neighbors. I felt contentment with the blending of laughter, my father's and mine.

The company for the Columbia Mine furnished a cabin for us: a cabin with a porch. Our nearest neighbor was at the small post office and general store, four miles away. The cabin had two rooms, so my parents occupied the bedroom and I had a cot near the iron stove in the larger room.

I can't remember ever hearing Mother speak about returning to California during those days in Bull Run. Neither can I remember any quarrels between my parents. Later I gathered her reasons for this change. Mother hadn't been eager to leave her job in Tuscarora but after the judge's son came down with scarlet fever, she began to be afraid for me. Then Dad promised, if she would agree to go with him to Bull Run, that she could handle the money and keep all she could save. As she put money away for our train trip, she must have felt she was on her way home at last.

We enjoyed more nights together around the bonfire. The happiness I connect with this time lingers in the fragrance of bacon cooking in the outdoors and the taste of crisp fried trout. Sometimes Dad would stretch his legs out on the ground and sing such songs as "Let the Rest of the World Roll By" or "Dear Old Girl." Sometimes Mom would tell stories about growing up on the sheep ranch. Smokey and Calico would curl up beside me and purr as if they, too, gloried in the unusual harmony.

Here, once again I found cherished solitude. I was old enough now to take short walks alone, and I must have walked along the sandy shore of the Bull Run River until I found a secret place where I could summon creativity in my unorthodox way.

Many times I've tried to remember the stories I whispered beside the river. I'm sure they must have had animals in them, but other than a vague memory of a beaver family and the elephant stories, I have no further recall. However, recently I decided to read some of the books I enjoyed as a child. I was startled to discover that many of the incidents I remembered from *Heidi* were not to be found. The tale of Heidi getting lost with her herd of goats and being rescued by Nemo, her shepherd dog, was missing. Nor could I find the story of Heidi coming to a party on The Sandy Shore. When I re-read Gene Stratton-Porter's books *The Keeper of the Bees* and *Girl of the Limberlost,* I made similar discoveries. I'd never wanted those books to end, so I must have done considerable plagiarizing of the characters for my imagination games.

We hadn't been in Bull Run very long before I started to reconstruct the life I'd known at The Divide. I named a new robin friend Red, after his predecessor; soon there were chipmunks with the names Nemo and Frisky, a rabbit called Peter, the second, and on and on until I'd drawn my animal family around me once more. It is small wonder that my memories of the two places became so difficult to separate.

Yet the landscape differed a great deal. That high desert country of The Divide, except for a few straggly pines and a thicket of cottonwood near Jack's Creek, had few trees. Mostly flat land, it was covered with sage and cow brush. Up at Bull Run, we were in the mountains. Even the air smelled different, like pine. A grove of aspen shook its silver leaves to invite walks of discovery. And the Bull Run River provided a song for the season.

Memories. Patches of sunlight in a dark forest. Each illuminated by an emotion: a bright ray of sorrow, joy, or fear slanting down on a scene.

One such scene occurred on an early morning when Dad asked if I'd like to see the beaver build their dam. "I came across their work crew yesterday."

When Dad mentioned "beaver," I couldn't get ready fast enough. Mother cautioned me to finish the oatmeal and not forget a sweater.

The air was that mixture of a cool fall morning wrapped in the promise of a warmer day. Smokey raced ahead of us through the wet grass after a gopher. Like a pianist, the river provided background music for this occasion, rippling its notes over the rocks.

After we left the forest of aspen trees to cut a path through the brush, Dad told me we must be very quiet so as not to disturb the workers or they'd walk off the job.

From time to time he stopped, finger to his lips.

Now he dropped down on one knee and made a small opening in the brush. The wild smell rushed out and awe took my breath.

I held Smokey close to keep him quiet while we peeked through the brush. If Dad had been showing me leprechauns, the astonishment could have been no greater.

A felled tree lay across the clearing with its leafy branches reaching into the river. I heard a sound like tiny saws; it was the beaver's long, sharp teeth gnawing on logs. A group of workers appeared to be making kindling out of a tree! Others in this assembly line swam in the pond that was forming behind the debris of wood. One group was making mud pies along the river's edge.

The brown, furry bodies weren't much larger than Smokey's,

but each wide, flat tail was as long again as the body. The flat tails slapped mud in place as the beavers stacked logs and rocks along the narrow bend in the river.

How I longed to reach out and touch those cuddly animals. I found the round, wise eyes above a curious, long nose and the tiny ears fascinating.

Later Dad told me the hind feet were webbed and that the second hind toe had a double claw so the animals were equipped for moving rocks and wood. They made a great deal of noise as they scurried about, sawing trees, diving into the water, and plopping mud with those flat tails.

I wanted to laugh out in delight. I looked up at Dad. His smile recognized the pleasure we shared.

And while I was content to remain frozen before this scene for as long as it lasted, Smokey grew restless and leaped from my arms crashing into the brush. A wild exodus from the beaver camp followed. Scampering, diving, splashing in all directions, they vanished. Silence.

Dad chuckled. "Now you know why people say, 'busy as a beaver.' Both ends of that animal work at once."

While we walked back to the cabin, Dad explained that the beaver built the dam to form a pool; it would be the front yard to their home. The rooms would open under water and be made of the same materials as the dam.

I was glad when he told me, "Those little fur pieces will be safe all winter from wolves, coyotes, and men."

When I asked what they ate, Dad said they were partial to aspen. "But they're not fussy and usually partake of water plants and such when their mama advises, 'Eat your vegetables.'"

I wanted to know where the babies were.

He explained that these were young beaver. When they're about two years old they leave their parents, who usually have younger children by then. In the spring the two-year-olds start out to build a new colony.

Most of the way home that day, I was quiet. Somewhere in the heart region I felt the familiar affinity to these wild creatures and recognized that same feeling in my father while he walked beside me.

Only the delivery of mail linked us to the outside world and mail delivery depended upon weather. Weeks went by without any outsider or messages invading our space. It's difficult to remember the silence over the land before radios, telephones, and freeways. Still I could always wake up excited by the possibility of a neighbor dropping in: a stray mountain lion, a hungry coyote, or perhaps a masked raccoon.

Distance, like time, can defy measurement. From our cabin to Tuscarora was said to be ninety-two miles but that equation failed to take in dirt roads, no roads at all, or weather that closed off any transportation for winter months. During severe weather no attempt was made to saddle horses and bring mail up the mountain. Bull Run Saloon, in a meadow some four miles from our cabin, served as general store, stage depot, and post office. Surrounding the saloon, the camp of Bull Run consisted of six or seven tents and cabins.

"Pony express. Here comes the pony express," the driver from the post office shouted on a November morning, as I—bundled in boots, mittens, fur cap, and the wool coat that Mom lined with various strips of animals pelts—raced to meet him. The way Mother's small eyes brightened, the way a slight frown drew her brows together always reminded me that mail could bring bad news as well as *St. Nicholas Magazine* and sometimes books, paper-dolls, and those awful, frilly dresses from my California aunt Ann Williford. Books, usually from Aunt Mary, were the best of these gifts. Usually Mom received letters from sisters Agnes, Kitty, and Ann. Sometimes there were notes and drawings for me from Mom's teenage sister, Mary, or from Aunt Bessie, the youngest of the McDonald clan.

Dad's only living relative was his sister, Aunt Minnie, married to William Hodges. Dad, a letter writer, received the most mail.

In the evenings after the arrival of mail, Mom and Dad talked to each other. That was one of the nicest things about mail delivery.

"Kitty writes that the strikes and union trouble are growing worse. She's worried about our brother, Bob; says someone planted a bomb in the machine shop where he works last week. He's being forced to join their union."

Such news infuriated Dad. His views on unions I would hear many times.

As I grew in awareness, hearing the same subject discussed I asked, "What are unions, Daddy?"

His answer I knew by heart. "It's a group of men who get together and tell other men what to do. They say, if you don't join our club and pay your dues, you can't work. Shouldn't be allowed in a free country."

Aunt Agnes wrote of union trouble among peach pickers in Selma, California, and of fruit rotting on trees. But one letter from my mother's brother Lockie praised the unions, "long as the fellows stick together, even us grease monkeys may get fair wages someday."

The great concern, other than unions, discussed in most letters from California was the war with Germany.

Mother would be sure to quote her brother-in-law on this subject. "Will Dunning says that those German U-boats are blowing up our ships faster than we can build them."

Mother's family looked up to Aunt Kitty's husband, Will

Dunning. Will was a dental technician, in business for himself. "A professional man," my mother said with pride.

Most of Mom's family belonged to the working class. Agnes's husband was a bartender before he became the owner of the peach ranch in Selma.

There was fearful talk of "the Huns."

"What does 'torpedoed' mean?" I would ask.

"Blown up. Blasted."

"Blasted? Like when you blast the mines with dynamite?"

Dad nodded. "Wilson's a dreamer," he said. "The big munitions plants bamboozled him into this war. As long as the country depends upon munitions for jobs, we'll have wars."

We will have wars!

"Are people going to—to shoot us?" I cried.

Mom's hand covered mine. "Not us, darling. Dad means America when he says 'we.' "

"Agnes worries that Warren may be drafted," she would go on. "How could she run the ranch alone?"

Mother's reassurance did little to diminish my fear. America? That meant the war was happening down there in California, didn't it? That was why my aunts sounded so worried. Now that someone had blasted the shop where Mother's brother worked, maybe she'd stop talking about wanting to return to California. Maybe we'd get to stay in Bull Run forever.

Magazines provided one of the happiest aspects of the mail. All three of us were insatiable readers. My loot included *Child's Companion, St. Nicholas, Little Pals,* and many animal stories. Dad and Mother received a variety of newspapers and magazines: *Saturday Evening Post, Woman's Home Companion,* and *Ladies' Home Journal,* among others.

Mother was reading a serial, Jack London's *Valley of the Moon,* that was running in one of these magazines. She said she loved it because it was set in California.

For weeks she talked about this story and I knew how eager she must be to read the second installment.

One afternoon, after the mail came, she and I sat out on the cabin porch to read.

Smokey slept near my feet, paying no attention to the chipmunks, which scurried in and out of their cage where there was food, water, and a miniature Ferris wheel. Smokey had learned it was a "no-no" to chase chipmunks.

I was talking to the chipmunks, when Red, our neighbor robin, darted down from the pine tree to flutter across the porch and make a terrible fuss.

This wasn't the first time. "A hawk!" I screamed.

Mother dropped her magazine and we ran inside for dish towels to wave in the air at the great circling hawk. When our robin's enemy departed and she returned to the babies in her nest, we looked for our magazines.

Then Mother shouted. For while we were rescuing Red, Haha had strolled over, and no doubt attracted by the strawberry color of Mom's magazine, picked it up off the ground, and with her big burro teeth chewed happily away.

"Give me that!" Mother cried. She ran after Haha and grabbed the edges of her magazine. Haha jerked it away. Mother snatched it back while I laughed at the tug of war. Then Mother made the mistake of getting her thumb in the way of Haha's teeth.

That was one of the rare times I saw her cry.

"Does it hurt awfully?" I asked, my tears rising up in sympathy.

"It hurts," she sobbed, holding her thumb. "But the w-worst of it is I'll never know what happened in the s-second installment."

Later the thumb turned blue then the nail dropped off. But that day I realized stories mattered as much to Mother as they did to me. I moved closer to her.

Time for a child plays its tunes on an accordion. For it is not months or years, but experience and impressions that stretch or shrink the minutes during growing years. So for me, at half past seven, it seemed we lived in Bull Run for years and years instead of a few months one fall. And the first two years at The Divide?

I had merged the earlier memories into the later ones under the file, My Mountain Home.

How can years be recognized when you've used up only seven? So in 1917 I drifted through August, September, October, and the first snow storms of November and came to think of that happiest period in my youth as "the *years* in Bull Run." For it to be no more than the three or four months that research proved it to be seems impossible! Events such as the singing of the river as it leap-frogged over rocks and boulders, the ever-present scent of pine mingled with stories whispered back by wind in the aspen, the lazy whir of insects interrupted by sass from a blue jay— these happenings fashioned a calendar more true than any recorded by scientific data.

I'd watched beaver pioneer a colony and caught the biggest trout in the Bull Run River while time stretched to its true dimension.

I was part of this place that let me be me—part of a large family that inhabited forests, water, and sky. If a sea creature were removed from the ocean to dry land, I guess he'd never again recognize who he was.

The Mud Wagon

As THIN, COLD AIR from the Independence Mountains moved north through Humboldt County, enveloping Bull Run in its sweep, the stars drew closer until they seemed as much a part of the landscape as the tree tops. I was going on eight that November of 1917 and liked to sit by the cabin window and wonder about the stars. Was each a small world? If not, why were they there? Only to be enjoyed like flowers?

One Friday night while I sat by the cabin window studying the skies, Dad slipped up behind me and put his hands on my shoulders. Softly he recited a poem:

> *He remembers those stars*
> *deep within him*
> *Stars by which he can steer*

Author's note: A mud wagon is also called a celerity or stage wagon. It is a type of vehicle that was used extensively during stage coaching days. More simply constructed than the Concord, it weighed up to one thousand pounds less than the coach and was built closer to the ground to reduce the danger of overturning. The mud wagon was slung on thorough braces rather than on main springs. Largely because of its light weight and low center of gravity, the vehicle was employed in mountain travel and over heavy roads. Nine passengers were accommodated inside. It was usually drawn with two or four horses or mules. Canvas side curtains could be drawn to suit prevailing weather conditions.

There are two restored mud wagons displayed at the Northeastern Nevada Museum in Elko. (Research courtesy of Howard Hickson, Northeastern Nevada Museum)

and grows impatient to be
on his way.

When I said I liked it, he promised to write it for me. "It's by an anonymous poet of Micronesia," he said, and he told me stories of people who lived much of their lives on the sea and used stars to find their way home.

"So when you discover those stars, you'll always know where you belong, Little Turk."

Later that night I woke up with a bad toothache. My jaw looked as if it were stuffed with candy chews. I knew I was too old to cry but that didn't stop me. I felt as if little men with spikes on their shoes jumped up and down inside my head. I even had a bad dream about the little men. I saw them sitting along the frame on the bottom of my bed, making grotesque faces and holding up the spiked shoes. Between pains I heard the cackle of their laughter.

Mother said I had a fever. She tried snow packs on my jaw, then oil of cloves that burned my mouth. Nothing helped.

"We've got to get her down to Tuscarora to the dentist," she told Dad.

"It's much too dangerous to attempt a trip down that grade," he protested. "Another storm's expected. I'll pull that tooth."

I screamed at the idea and refused to open my mouth.

At day break Dad saddled Dolly and went for his friend, Huddleson.

Only the day didn't break. The sky was an ominous black and snow kept falling. Dad and Huddleson returned with the sled and the four of us slid and swerved over snow, across the meadow and down the slope to the post office and general store where the stage stopped.

The store wasn't open at this early hour and we had to stand outside, teeth chattering, and wait a long, long time for the stage coach. Most of the time I kept my face pressed against my mother's coat.

Just before that small mud wagon arrived I looked up to caution Dad to be sure and feed Smokey and Calico and not to forget the squirrels and chipmunks and to put crumbs out for the robins.

Dad chuckled. "Don't worry, honey, I'll take care of the cats and all our boarders."

At the last minute, tall, lanky Buck Horn arrived, opened his store, and brought out mail sacks to toss into the rear boot of the mud wagon. Four horses pulled the wagon.

Buck sympathized with me, told Dad he had to go down to Elko for supplies, and promised to look out for us. Mother and I sat in the back with a thin buggy robe over us. Buck fastened the canvas curtains on the sides before swinging himself up on the front seat beside the driver, rifle across his knees, to ride "shotgun."

The driver, I learned later, was part Paiute Indian, part Mexican. Everyone called him "Pie." Straight black hair hung down over his collar from under an orange knit cap that covered his ears. The orange tassel on top bobbed when he turned his head. A dark beard and sideburns covered sunken cheeks. His jaws moved steadily chewing tobacco but he seldom spoke, except to Buck Hopper who understood Indian dialect.

"Pie says we're going to run into some bad stuff tonight," Buck said as he got in. "Hope it doesn't get worse before we get down off the grade."

Pie shouted to the horses and the two leads, tawny Rum and skinny Toddy, strained against their collars and we were off down the mountain.

With the swaying of the coach, continuous creaking, frequent bounces, and the rhythmic flap of the canvas curtains, I curled closer to Mom, and, shivering, fell asleep.

The pain in my jaw woke me and I heard the hail beating down on the canvas and knew the dreaded storm had arrived.

Wind tore the curtains loose and blew across the back seat in icy gusts. Mother covered my face with her wool scarf. I felt her tense each time the coach jerked and swayed.

I heard Buck call to explain to Mother about storms growing to the point where the driver couldn't see the road. Then he loosened the reins and trusted the horses to get us down safely.

Poles, ten feet high called snow stakes, marked the sides of the narrow road. Sometimes snow covered the poles as they did that night. Now and then, the top of a snow stake, orange as Pie's hat, emerged from the snow.

I remembered Dad's poem and guessed the horses had those stars within them to steer by.

Snow was blowing into the wagon and it seemed we were taking the turns at a terrific speed. Suddenly the coach careened one way, then away over to the other side before I felt it go over. It was the strangest feeling, unreal, rather than frightening at first: a sensation of rolling, then sinking, sinking into white, icy nothingness.

I heard Mother's muffled scream. "Where is she? Oh, God! Shirley, where are you?"

Her fear transferred to me. Frantically I dug through snow. I couldn't call and I couldn't get out. I panicked. Finally Buck reached me and lifted me out of the snow bank. Crying, Mom put her arms around me.

Pie and Buck turned the mud wagon back up on its runners. Helping me up on the seat, Mother climbed in beside me. Wind whipped through my wet clothing and I was so cold I couldn't feel the throbbing tooth.

Pie shouted a lot of bad words at the horses. Mom covered my ears. Buck took off his coat and insisted on putting it around me. Once more we started down and around the steep curves.

Finally we crossed the flatland into the familiar mining camp of Tuscarora. Ugly makeshift houses, tawdry saloons, weeds, outhouses, and wooden sidewalks were mercifully concealed that evening beneath the frosting of snow. Smoke curled upward from chimneys.

"We'll stop at the post office," Mom called to Buck. "Dora La Marr may have room for us."

Dora, the postmistress, gave us the same rooms we'd had before. But she shook her head when Mom asked about a dentist.

There were no dentists in town. We could wait for a visiting dentist or we could take the stage on to Elko.

Most folks in Tuscarora, she explained, used home remedies. So before the night was over, Dora had tied a string around my aching tooth, attached the other end to the door knob, and proceeded to slam the door. I tasted blood while my tongue found a large, vacant place in my mouth. The pain was gone.

In our family we were not unfamiliar with home remedies. We kept a flask of whiskey for snake bites. I was never certain whether you put the whiskey on the bite or drank it. Baking soda served for both indigestion and tooth paste. Mom was a great believer in poultices and whether it was a sliver too deep for a needle or a chest cold, she applied a poultice of either bread and milk or flaxseed. The flaxseed was purchased in sacks and had other uses: a dependable laxative or water softener, it was most often used in our house after blasting to remove dust particles from the eye. Mom would hold down my lower lashes while she inserted a single seed in the corner of my eye. "It will travel all around like a little boat," she always said, "and any unwanted particle will stick to it."

The flaxseed remedy gave quick relief without pain, which was more than I could say for Dora's method of pulling teeth.

An era in my life closed that night. I didn't know that I would not return to Bull Run, nor did I realize that a wedge of time I had known was slipping into a past that would be remembered as "colorful," a time already gone for most of the country.

By that late fall of 1917, remnants of the fast-fading frontier remained only in remote places such as northern Nevada. I was seeing the rag-tag ends of a time when women carried water from rivers and creeks; the last of kerosene lamps, blacksmith shops, and outhouses; and soon we would see the old stage coaches and mud wagons only in Western movies.

Spies

A FEW DAYS AFTER our return to Tuscarora, we moved into the boarding house where Mom had worked, this time as guests. After the frightening experience in the mud wagon, Mom decided it was too late in the year for us to return to Bull Run. She vowed she'd never spend another winter in an isolated cabin.

Mom had other ideas. She had been saving Dad's wages for the last three months, and he had promised she could "go to California for a visit over Christmas." When speaking of our trip to California, Dad always said "for a visit," while Mom said, "when we return home."

I just couldn't imagine not returning to Bull Run, and I fully expected we would be back there next spring.

In Tuscarora few changes had taken place at the boarding house. A Chinese male cook replaced Mother. Meanie, the frail and shriveled Indian woman, still crouched behind the stove with her rice bowl.

Best of all, the school term was well underway so I was not sent back to the dreaded schoolhouse.

But I had other worries. Once more Mom became busy washing and ironing clothes to pack, and I feared that, this time, we really might be going to California. Sometimes she hummed little tunes to herself and I heard her laugh more frequently.

Then a few weeks after our arrival, Dad returned to be welcomed back by his many friends at the boarding house. He had found a backer for his mines and would return to The Divide.

One night he sat in the after-dinner poker game. With the intention of doubling Mother's small hoard, he lost the train fare to her freedom. The threat of California, for me, ended that night but so did our peaceful interlude. At first I heard their angry voices at night, then the daytime silences followed.

Dad's popularity with the three women who had come down from the mines to winter in town won him no favors from Mom. When he strolled through the parlor, the three women stopped knitting as he always had a few quips or stories—"suitable for the ladies."

One afternoon, after commending them on knitting for the soldier boys, he asked how many ladies put their names in the package. All three nodded.

"One sentimental young lady," Dad told them recounting a piece that appeared in the *Elko Independent* where he must have read it, "put her card in socks knit for soldiers overseas and got the following reply:

> *Sox received. A perfect fit.*
> *One is a helmet, the other a mitt.*
> *I hope we meet when I've done my bit*
> *but who in hell taught you to knit?*

And Dad went out followed by laughter, admiring gazes, and remarks. "Ped's a card, isn't he?"

"What a disposition! Must be a joy to live with."

The ladies looked at Mom. She remained silent, her lips stern, her eyes intent on her magazine: another installment of Jack London's *Valley of the Moon*.

Soon Mom was cooking for the boarders, who had grown weary of chow mein. Every night around the long table, the boarders discussed the daily news. Newspapers were sacrosanct in those pre-radio days and the populace of our small mining community, having had little exposure to propaganda, believed the *Elko Independent* as I believed in the "Little Nemo" comic strip. No sympathy would be expressed for a pacifist preacher who, according to the *Elko Independent,* "was horsewhipped by a Kentucky band and beaten unmercifully. The gang, it was believed, organized to punish pacifists."

Dad had been warned by Mother not to express his anti-war views. In Tuscarora, he was in the minority and Mom might have feared for her job. I worried nightly over what he might say that would show us to be "different."

On the night when someone read from the paper that Washington, D.C., had gone dry at midnight October thirty-first, Dad joined with the majority of independent citizens who bellowed disapproval. The town supported five saloons.

The talk around the dining table that intrigued me most at the time concerned spies. The following editorial in the *Elko Independent* started a discussion concerning German spies in America: "Spies," the editorial advised, "are watching our faces. They look for signs of moral weakness. If the spies spot such signs, they'll figure our morale is breaking under strain of war and they are winning."

Spies in our town! Did Antoine know this?

"I never heard such poppycock!" Dad would exclaim. Then he would go into one of his tirades about propaganda from Washington where such fiction was brewed to desensitize people and keep them buying bonds to support munitions factories.

Disapproving silence at the table followed his outburst. I studied my napkin and wished, for once, that Dad wore a small flag in his buttonhole.

Then one man quietly explained to Dad that if the story wasn't true, it wouldn't have appeared in the *Elko Independent.*

Dad snorted but said no more. Maybe Mom pinched him under the table.

I made up stories about spies and liked to pretend I was spying on people in the boarding house.

Once Mom burst into our room and caught me whispering rapidly, while I shook a spy story out of a corner of the sheet.

I attempted to smooth out the sheet in a casual manner. Usually when I'd been jerked out of a story it took a little time to become oriented.

Mom frowned, looking at me intently. "What are you doing up here alone? Who were you talking to?"

She made it sound like being alone was something questionable.

"To—to Smokey." I glanced for collaboration at my black friend on the foot of the bed but his attention was engaged by a flea.

She suggested I run along outside and play with my friends. That day I heard the annoyance in her voice.

Both of us were aware that I didn't know anyone, except Antoine, in Tuscarora. But since it made Mom happy to pretend, I went outside to walk with my thoughts of intrigue and spies. I'm sure I longed for that welcoming solitude of The Sandy Shore.

Eventually, Dad must have found the stories of spies in Tuscarora amusing; for later he added these stories to his fund of anecdotes to entertain my mother's family. He entertained me with stories, too, during the time we spent in town together.

During those cold November days while he and I strolled along, our feet plop-plopping on the broken wooden sidewalks, pausing while he chatted with Mrs. Rose at the General Store or with Dora La Marr at the post office, or with the Primeauxs, the talk was mostly of spies.

"It is our patriotic duty to appear cheerful," Mrs. Rose, at the grocery store told us with repeated nods of her head, while she took a butterball out of the apothecary jar for me.

In Buck Horn's saloon, where I sat on a high stool drinking hot chocolate, the following heated discussion was one that I heard Dad repeat many times.

Buck would rage about old Willhelmstraser who had hired psychologists with two-ton brains to watch our people.

Dad wanted to know where these heavy-headed watchers were supposed to be staked out.

I must have squirmed on the bar stool, hoping Dad wasn't going to argue and let everyone know he was not patriotic. It was bad enough that he never went to church or wore that tiny flag on his coat.

"New York, San Francisco, Washington," Buck supplied, sliding a mug of beer across the bar to Dad. "Wouldn't surprise me none if there were some right here in town."

Buck's brother, Barney, informed us that the spies were watching the president. "He damn well better appear cheerful."

The consensus was if the spies reported Americans dragging their feet "—flat and fishy-eyed—" as Buck put it, that would be the Germans' clue to redouble efforts with their submarines.

"Yep," another beer guzzler agreed. "If the watchers find us keyed up and capable, the war is won."

I remember Dad's chuckle because everyone spun around as if they were mad at him. I nearly spilled my chocolate.

"What the devil are you laughin' about, Ped?" Buck asked.

"Just appearing cheerful, Buck. Helping to win the war," Dad replied.

I must have sighed relief.

For a time the town was full of unnatural smiles. Dora La Marr, habitually solemn, would suddenly remember in the midst of a conversation to twist up the corner of her wide mouth.

Mrs. Rose, who took care of everybody's business along with each grocery order, never allowed customers to forget. With a display of horsey teeth, she would shake a finger and whisper, "Remember somebody may be watchin'."

Antoine and I talked about it. If there were spies in Tuscarora, who could they be? Was it old Meanie, the Indian woman watching and listening from behind the stove? Antoine thought the Chinese laundry man a good suspect.

The grins and reminders lasted throughout the month, but by December people settled into the grim reality of another Nevada winter.

Francis Primeaux, who knew many influential people in Elko, told Mom about a possible job there. Mom brightened. Elko would be the first leg in her journey back to California.

I'd heard her say many times she wished she'd trained to be a nurse. Practical, capable, and strong, she would have made a good one.

Francis told Mom there was a piece in the *Elko Independent* about a new hospital opening and suggested they may need nurses.

~

In 1987 when I returned to Elko to do some research for this story in newspapers of 1917 and 1918, I came across the following piece:

> *Mrs. C. J. Littlefield and Margaret Weeks have opened a private hospital in the Littlefield residence on Pine Street and have fitted up her home with eight beds. . . . Since the Boling Hospital was closed early last summer, Elko has been without a hospital and the two nurses should receive the support of the entire community in this venture.*

I had the strangest feeling that it was 1917 and I was looking at that paper through my mother's eyes. She would be picturing herself in a white uniform and cap. Such a profession would give her the dignity she longed for.

The newsprint blurred for a moment. I felt her nervousness about applying for the job, felt her replace it with her usual determination.

And how did I feel at the time? My feelings must have been mixed. In one way I wanted Mom to get the job she wanted so much. Yet I was deeply troubled over leaving Dad and our mountain home. Mom never spoke about returning. Maybe we were leaving forever. I didn't dare to think about another strange school or what might happen to us in Elko.

The Sugar Bowl
1917

W E'LL BE ON THE stagecoach a good part of the day," Mother told me. She explained it was a forty-mile drive to Elko and advised me to take a book or a doll to play with.

Although I would be eight years old the approaching March, Mother hadn't guessed that I only played with dolls to please her. I liked my playmates warm and alive. "I'll just take Smokey."

Mother explained the rules. Smokey must travel in a box and ride with the luggage on top of the stagecoach.

This information distressed me greatly. Poor Smokey would be scared, jolting around in a strange place without me to reassure him. It was just as well that Mom hadn't let me bring Calico. Dad promised to take care of my kitten. He said he'd try to come and see us at Christmas.

The thought of Christmas, only two weeks off, increased my loneliness. I glanced at Mom. She held the *Elko Independent* with the advertisement for a practical nurse in her lap and had the look of being far away from the mud wagon, the moment, and me.

Four horses drew the mud wagon, which, besides Mom and me, carried three local men. Two young miners sat in the rear with us; an older man who was a sheriff in Elko rode "shotgun" with the driver. In order to avoid being delayed by the freight team, the mud wagon took the upper route from Tuscarora, a rough road circling the low hills. Meanwhile the freight team cut straight

Mother and I in San Francisco, 1910. (William Norin)

At eighteen months of age, I'm sitting with my cat Smokey in Hanford, California, in 1911. (William Norin)

Our cabin at The Divide, front and rear view, still standing when I revisited it in 1991, when these pictures were taken. (Gary Hacker)

I'm standing by an old mine shaft in The Divide. (Gary Hacker)

Our outhouse still stands after almost 75 years—no glass door knobs here. (Gary Hacker)

A stagecoach like the one that delivered Mother and I to Tuscarora. (Northeastern Historical Society, Elko Museum)

An un-covered wagon outside of Elko. (Northeastern Historical Society, Elko Museum)

It's 1917 and I'm 7 years old, standing behind Buck Horn who's holding Antoine Primeaux (6 years) and Pat Primeaux (4 years).

Stagecoach in front of the Miner's Hotel, Tuscarora, 1906. (Northeastern Historical Society, Elko Museum)

My mother, Teresa Pedlar, photographed in Berkeley, 1920.

Cousin Helen and Aunt
Kitty Dunning, 1938.
(William Norin)

Mother (center)
poses with two of
her sisters: Aunt
Bessie (left) and
Aunt Williford.
(William Norin)

A family outing at Neptune Beach in Alameda around 1915: Aunt Williford, wearing a white dress and no hat, is sitting on the rail; Alfred Williford is the man kneeling on the left and Will Dunning, wearing a cap, is kneeling next to him; behind Will is Aunt Mary, standing with no hat; and behind her is Kitty Dunning, the last woman on the rail on the right. (William Norin)

"Fanchon's Fancies," a daily fashion column in a San Francisco newspaper, featured the creations of the dancer Fanchon, of Fanchon and Marco Theatrical Company. I later toured with Fanchon and Marco as a professional dancer.

across the valley. This team of sixteen horses pulled several wagons lashed together, a less expensive method of bringing ore down from the mines than paying exorbitant rail rates.

Every eight miles, about every four hours, horses were changed. At Lone Mt. Station, Reed Station, Eagle Drop Stage Stop, and other hospitality and rest stations, we would be offered hash and pie, while the men—no doubt enjoying a nip of old Barleycorn on the Q.T.—gathered around the stables where horses were changed. Some of the stations had blacksmiths and I never tired of watching horses get new shoes.

Each time the stagecoach stopped, I asked the driver if I could see Smokey. A kind man, who like most locals knew my father, held me up so I could console my crying cat. He filled Smokey's water bowl and I was allowed to share bits of my lunch. But Smokey wasn't hungry. His eyelids stretched with terror. I knew that he, too, longed for the freedom and security surrounding a small cabin in the humming silence of the mountains.

When I thought about the mountains, I made abortive attempts to write in my notebook. It was for my Dad that I struggled to put words on paper. For myself it was enough to whisper stories in solitude. In my great admiration for my father, I hoped to make him notice me. Not that he ever ignored me. But I was aware that he, like me, lived an absorbing inner life that needed no one for long periods of time. I feared that he might forget me, the same as I often mislaid my treasures. So when we were separated, I lived in fear that he might never return.

The stories, like nature, were a bond between us. Dad, a constant reader, always showed interest in what I'd been writing. So, while the stage coach jolted along, I clutched a stubby pencil in my small fingers and tried to force churning thoughts into difficult words. My fingers never learned to move fast enough and I felt the elusive wonder melt away before it could reach paper.

On the stagecoach that day, I remembered the times down on the river bank when I'd helped Dad pan for gold; how I'd loved to watch the quick silver in the small frying pan split and dart to gather gold flakes from the ore. My words on the paper were like the gray gravel with all bright color lost. Later I learned this was a dilemma of most writers.

Sounds of horses' hooves and creaking wheels as we bounced over rutted roads broke the desert silence. Rolling knolls swept out in all directions, tucking in small valleys between hillocks dotted with snow-frosted sage, yellow rabbit brush, and green mule brush. The thin afternoon sun erased cloud patterns from the hills then brushed the sage with water colors, blending shades of mauve, violet, and ochre.

The next day in Elko was a gray one. I waited in a rooming house with Smokey while Mother went for the interview. When she returned I could see that, although she had a job, she was disappointed. After learning that Mom had run a boarding house in Tuscarora, Mrs. Little hired her as a cook, not a nurse in the new hospital.

We moved into a two-room cottage behind the spacious home that Mrs. Little had converted into Elko's Hospital. Mom nearly lost the job when Mrs. Little learned I owned a cat. An indispensable cat. Mom warned me to keep Smokey from ever entering the hospital. He must remain inside the cottage except when I took him out with me.

"It will only be for a short time," Mother promised. "One day soon, you'll have a nice home with a big yard to play in."

The cottage behind the hospital seemed spacious compared to our cabin at The Divide. One room served as bedroom and living room, with a closet-sized kitchen. A back entrance led to the outhouse. One advantage, according to Mom, was the location. I could walk to school.

To my relief, school was out for Christmas holidays. But that was the only happy thing about Christmas that year. Dad wrote that he must postpone his visit for a few weeks. He wanted to wait until there was enough ore to take to the assayer, so he needn't make more than one trip down the mountain. Mom said he probably didn't have the stage-coach fare.

She put a tiny tree in our room and I decorated it with the stars I cut out of silver paper and strings of popcorn. My California aunts sent the fancy dresses and dolls that I hardly cared to unwrap. But I brightened upon opening a copy of *Black Beauty* by Anna Sewell, a gift from Aunt Mary, my mother's younger sister. How well I remember that feeling of happy expectation a new book brought—especially a book about an animal!

But I couldn't always escape in a book. I was aware of how hard Mom worked. I worried about her. And when school started in January, I had more worries. All I wanted was to blend into my class. But from the first day, even though I appeared in a wool jumper looking similar to other girls, I was pointed out as being "different." It happened when the teacher read my address aloud; I became "the girl who lives in the hospital." In that school, much larger than the one-room schoolhouse in Tuscarora, I failed to make friends. I became a loner.

Around that time, when I needed them most, my stories deserted me. Sometimes, while Mother cooked, served meals—mostly on trays—and even did some cleaning, I stayed in our quarters and sought comfort in The Wad. Sitting on the bed, with a corner of the sheet or blanket squeezed in both hands, I tried to summon the wonderful elephant or beckon Heidi. But it was useless. Nothing happened. Escape was impossible.

Gray days stretched into weeks. Inside the hospital, I was no more welcome than Smokey. The rules were never to run in the halls, never to talk out loud or enter a patient's room. For a child who had raced after squirrels, splashed in the river, and scrambled up pines to investigate bird nests, this restricted life seemed unbearable. Not wanting to add to Mother's burden I shared my tears with Smokey.

The hospital smelled of antiseptic and sickness. Carts of trays stood with partly-eaten food on slippery linoleum floors. Shrieks of pain sounded at intervals, as did unrestrained sobbing, but when Mrs. Pitman, who Mom said was "sick in the head," released piercing screams I covered my ears.

Once Smokey followed me into the hospital corridor when I had something to tell Mother. Mrs. Little was angry and Mom warned me that she might lose her job if it ever happened again.

I'm sure Mrs. Little must have been a fine woman to want to open a hospital and care for people. I remember only her cross voice and stern face.

If there was one redeeming feature in Elko for me, it was the movie house. Mother gave me a dime and let me go every Saturday to the matinee. I'm certain she must have been grateful for that movie house. I found comfort in watching someone else's stories in pictures and a challenge in reading the titles quickly before they flashed off the screen. There I first saw Pavlowa with the entire Ballet Russe in *The Dumb Girl of Portica*. I dreamed of myself in a white ballet tutu with silver glitter. I made up music and started to set steps to it. I'm not certain if my father's theory of something mystical existing in the act of matching body movements to music had anything to do with my love of dancing. For a time it filled the loss of story telling.

Another children's matinee featured one of my favorite books, *Girl of the Limberlost* by Gene Stratton-Porter. But such films were soon replaced by many war propaganda movies such as *The Fall of the Nation* and *Patria*. Real pathos with Victor Herbert's music and many Hollywood stars emphasized the theme that the defeat of the defense bill before Congress could cause disaster. I could hear my Dad say the public was being brainwashed.

Newsreels reported the Bolsheviks were in control of Russia. While pictures showed Russian soldiers fighting the Germans in a blizzard, a pianist played sad music. Titles explained that men were starving.

Nearing the end of February Congress introduced an eight-hour work law for women, but Mother said it was unlikely to affect Elko or her job.

Then on the first of March, two weeks before my birthday, something happened to change our lives. Mother's friend Mrs. Francis Primeaux with her two sons, Antoine and Pat, arrived by stagecoach from Tuscarora. I'd missed Antoine and was glad to see him. Both boys looked elegant in tweed knickers, white shirts, and knee-high socks stretched over their sturdy calves. Antoine's fair hair was sun-bleached. His cheeks were round and ruddy, his brown eyes curious and friendly as a chipmunk.

Mrs. Primeaux suggested we run out and play. She counseled the boys to try and stay clean.

I knew that she and Mother, seated around the tiny table in the kitchen, wanted to talk about something in private. Having a day off at the hospital, Mother had cooked a jack-rabbit stew for our guests. The *Elko Independent* urged housewives to be patriotic during a meat shortage and cook jack rabbits to save meat for "our brave soldier boys."

But that day with other things on my mind, I had no appetite. I'd made a discovery that I was eager to show Antoine. A short distance from Mrs. Little's Hospital on the fringe of town, I'd seen a long abandoned, covered wagon. Some of the kids from school gathered there to play Indians and immigrants.

I wanted to see the inside of the wagon and longed to be included in the games.

"Don't you know these kids?" Antoine asked me as we ran through snow toward the wagon.

Smokey, as always, was at my heels.

Before I could answer, two of the boys in my grade stuck their heads out the rear of the wagon. "What's she doing here?" one asked.

"We want to see the wagon," Antoine replied.

The boys looked at one another. I'd never seen anyone refuse

Antoine anything. He had a friendly grin and seemed to take his welcome for granted.

"You can come," one boy said. "But we don't want her in here."

A girl with straw-colored pigtails stuck her head out through the back slit in the canvas and said "Hi," to the boys, then she said something like, "We don't want her. Is she sick or something? She lives at the hospital."

"That's not nice, Ellen May," Antoine told her. "Open the canvas. We're coming in."

"We're coming in." Pat always echoed Antoine.

Antoine scrambled up into the rear of the wagon and pulled me in through the shreds of canvas.

Thus it was that he installed me among my peers. Convinced that I was normal and healthy, I was admitted through the torn curtain. Inside "the immigrants" lunched on cookies.

We were told that Antoine and I could be good immigrants, but Pat had to be a bad Indian to even up numbers. He seemed pleased. Actually he looked like an Indian with his straight black hair standing straight up. And he often acted savage. Happiness was mine that afternoon. Antoine was my friend. I belonged.

With wild war whoops the Indians arrived. One of the boys drove the covered wagon with the pretend horses at top speed. Others aimed sticks out the back, and from under the sides of the canvas we bang-banged the enemy. The Indians were after our scalps and, when captured, we rolled in the snow, yelping and screaming. When the game broke up I called and called to Smokey. Finally he came, a black streak bounding over the snow-frosted sage.

It was a day of broadening horizons for both of us. I had new playmates. Smokey discovered desert space to roam in. Not as great as our mountains with trees and river, still better than town streets. Here was a great place for both of us. Or so it seemed that afternoon.

My mother gasped when we walked in. The boys were wet, dirty, and covered with stickers. I didn't look any better, but Mother's concern centered on the boys.

Francis Primeaux laughed. I thought she was very nice about it, suggesting children couldn't keep clean and have fun. "So we'll shock the travelers on the coach." Her dimples suggested she enjoyed shocking people.

Sometimes I wondered how it would be if my family were important like the Primeauxs. Mrs. Primeaux had help to cook and to clean her house. Whenever she came to town to stay at the best hotel, an item in the Elko papers heralded the event.

Yet she had chosen my hard-working mother for a friend. Both had dark brown hair, long and heavy textured, worn in a bun. Both had fair English skin. Mother could claim the prettiest mouth while her friend looked at the world with merry, brown eyes. Perhaps both recognized the steel behind the femininity in the other. Gold towns, like Tuscarora, were no place for sissies.

When we were washed and brushed up for lunch, I wondered about the conversation between Mom and Francis Primeaux, for my mother appeared happier than I'd seen her for a long time. And so was I.

Before leaving, Mrs. Primeaux mentioned that a Mrs. Briggs would be expecting Mother the next day.

Later I asked Mother who Mrs. Briggs was.

"It's a secret," she said, with her happy smile, and added that she might have a surprise for me.

Mother's surprises hadn't been good ones for a long, long time. Did this mean we were going to move again? Unless we returned to the mountains, I didn't want to risk another move. I'd been accepted by some of my schoolmates that day. Maybe, even without Antoine, they might let me play immigrants in the mysterious wagon. The idea of another strange place and new school made my stomach hurt.

That night I used hot match sticks to remove the ticks in Smokey's skin. Dad had shown me how the quick touch of a hot match stick made the tick back out until it could be removed with a turn or two. I told Smokey not to worry about moving. "Maybe we'll stay here for awhile and you can play on the desert."

But I could hear Mother singing as she cleaned up the kitchen, and I didn't confide my apprehension in Smokey.

What I most feared came true. We were to move again. But as it turned out, I was overjoyed to learn we were leaving the hospital for good! Mom wasn't to work there any longer. The new house was only a few blocks from my school, and, bad as it was, I guessed a new school might be worse.

The house, a two-story building across from Elko High School, had been remodeled as a dormitory for a proposed junior college. But with war having priority over education, tax money went for tanks and ammunition.

Architecturally, our dorm house was original to say the least and, Mother decided, perfect for a boarding house. The downstairs boasted a large kitchen and one enormous dining room off a long entry hall. The former parlor and downstairs bedroom vanished into the all-important dining room. Upstairs eight cubicle bedrooms clustered with a certain wistfulness around the one bathroom. Had it become a dorm, the pandemonium on a school morning exceeded imagination!

For Mother—and for me in a lesser degree—the house possessed the attributes of a palace. Compared to our cabins, this tall, skinny house was extravagantly endowed with running water, toilet, actual chairs instead of camp stools, and a no-draft, snake-proof floor. Compared to Mrs. Little's hospital, the dorm house offered freedom. Independence meant even more to Mother than convenience and luxury. And that was a great deal as she longed for a more gracious way of life—the longing of a little girl raised on a sheep ranch and never knowing anything except hardship and endless work.

So in that spring of 1918, she embarked upon plans to give me a birthday party—something I'd never had with guests other than squirrels. Even as I write I can feel the sadness of her situation, for with all her loving, stubborn Scottish heart she was determined that her child would have the best this world could offer.

Ironically, for the child that meant the wilderness.

A week after we'd moved in, Mother had four boarders and only two vacancies. News that she "spread a good table" passed from tongue to tongue and Mother could be choosy. Two young schoolteachers from the high school occupied the choice front bedrooms—if those cubicles could be granted the status of that name. Mr. Stokely, an elderly man, and a Mrs. Fields, a fussy old lady, rented side rooms with little view. These boarders, I'd heard, were someone's in-laws, deposited—no doubt with relief—in Mother's care.

With this income, Mother set about creating "a home where you can be proud to entertain your friends." That the home consisted of one gigantic oblong of a dining room left Mother undaunted. Soon a sofa moved into the space beneath the bay window. A Queen Ann table, rescued from a secondhand shop and then sanded and polished, reigned over a gray rabbit-skin rug. The latter, a constant reminder of live bunnies, depressed me but I never told Mother.

At that time she wrote ecstatic letters to her sisters in the San Francisco Bay area: a few were preserved and helped fill in memory gaps. She described the house as having eight bedrooms, neglecting to mention the size. She wrote of her efforts to beautify the dining room for the big event—my March birthday party.

The sisters decided to send a housewarming gift. And, as Mother's letters suggested that her favorite room was one for dining, what better gift than fine china? So boxes of Haviland arrived with their many stamps: Fragile; Handle with care.

I can still see my mother's fingers as she turned the graceful sugar bowl around and around, while releasing small sighs of pleasure. The china, patterned in a wild-rose design, was never used on that long, boarding-house table. For with all her longing for frivolity, necessity taught Mother to be practical.

As far as the birthday party went, I wanted ordinary plates like I'd seen at other parties. I would sooner have used our cracked plates from the cabin than to flaunt Haviland and give my peers the wrong impression. It was equally shameful to appear overly rich or poor.

Mother had a dilemma. She couldn't bear to leave her precious dishes in the box, put away until a sixteenth birthday. She solved the problem by providing plate rails. Fortunately, the boarder, Mr. Stokely, having been a carpenter, offered his services in exchange for a week's room and board. Soon a graceful, cream-colored railing ran around three walls. Mother left the large plates packed, while she decorated the room with the smaller pieces. She highlighted the pinks and greens in the dishes with matching pillows and a large picture of *The Three Graces,* which Mrs. Fields protested was "unfitting, those undressed ladies flitting about!" Tongue clicking followed these words.

Then, two weeks before the party, it happened. Roused from deep sleep, I heard a racket downstairs. Intermittent crashes and a weird howling mingled with a soft pouncing sound. Loud, excited voices brought me scrambling down the stairs.

Our boarders, all in an apparent hysterical state, crowded the small entry. At my appearance, all eyes fixed on me and a silence, more ominous than the noise in the dining room, fell on the narrow hall.

Instantly Mother was at my side and if I'd harbored any doubts as to a tragedy, they were dispelled by her crushing embrace. Then she whirled to face her boarders. "Please everyone step outside." Her tone suggested that they should have known enough to leave us alone.

"What's in there?" I made a move toward the dining room and Mother held me tighter.

"You can't go in there, darling," she whispered and her voice broke. Her deep-set eyes were watery. Mother never cried.

"What's in there?" My imagination leaped from dragons to wild animals. I thought I heard the cry of a tiger.

Then what she told me was worse by far than any horrors I could imagine.

"It's—Smokey," she said. "He's sick, sweetheart."

I pulled away from her in panic. "Let me get him!"

Mother explained that Smokey had rabies. There had been an outbreak in the county. Some wild animal must have bitten my cat out on the desert. She didn't dare open the dining room door for Smokey was out of his head and if he bit me, I'd get this deadly disease.

I asked Mom if she had called the doctor.

"You must be very brave," Mother told me. "No one can save Smokey. He will have to be destroyed."

I stared at my mother and whatever it was that she saw in my eyes started a real flood of tears from hers. "Come," she suggested we take a walk until the sheriff had left.

"Sheriff?" I was too stunned to cry. This couldn't be happening. It was only a bad dream. "What can the sheriff do?"

Again Mother whispered that word, *destroy.*

And, there he was, the big man wearing a broad-rimmed hat, a star on his coat and a holster around his waist.

From inside, as if he sensed the arrival, Smokey let out a protesting howl. I saw the man's hand move to the holster and I screamed.

Next to snakes, there was nothing I feared as much as guns.

The sheriff suggested to Mom that she take me outdoors. Then he tried to reassure me that my cat wouldn't suffer. "Just put him out of his misery, see?"

I remember not being able to take my eyes off his gun. How I must have longed to break into that dining room and hold Smokey in my arms. Surely he would stop leaping and howling in that scary way if I could hold him.

"Please. Please . . ." I kept saying the one word over and over.

Mother tried to persuade me to walk with her out of hearing of the shots. But there in the front yard, I was rooted in my pain. Then the shots exploded inside of me. Both of them. They blasted in my ears so for a time I couldn't hear. Shards of pain pierced my chest.

Mother attempted to hide my face in her dress, but not before I saw the sheriff come down the steps holding the small black body by the back of the neck.

The loss became real then. I sobbed until I lost my breath and got sick. The crying spells went on for lonely days without my closest playmate. I refused to go into that dining room and ate my meals in my bedroom or the kitchen. The first glimpse of that room immediately after the event turned it into a chamber of horrors, for amongst the clutter of smashed Haviland, blood stained the plate rail. Even after Mr. Stokely applied a fresh coat of paint, I refused to go in.

A week later we had my party. I didn't want a party. But invitations had been sent. Mother talked brightly and tried unsuccessfully to work up my enthusiasm. So I wore the pink organdy dress that the aunts had sent. The company, the cake, the gifts meant nothing.

A birthday gift arrived from my Dad with a letter promising he'd come soon. The gift was a collar he'd made for Smokey.

I was far too centered in my grief to consider my mother's loss until I heard one of the boarders say, "I know how dreadful you must feel about your beautiful china."

On the day of the party, I forced myself for Mom's sake to enter that hateful dining room. When I glanced up at the plate rail, I saw she'd decorated it with crepe paper pom-poms.

The next day I found Mom kneeling beside a newspaper with pieces of the sugar bowl. She was gluing them together. For a few moments I experienced something of her disappointment: not the china alone as much as she loved it, not the disappointment of the long-planned birthday party, but a home for gracious living that she hoped to provide for me. Two gun shots had wiped those hopes out forever.

"There," she said holding up the sugar bowl with a jagged hole under the handle. "It won't be the way it was, but it's the best I can do."

I dropped down on my knees beside her and after we'd cried together, I felt better. Somewhere, deep down, beyond anything I could put in words, I knew my brave mother had mended more than a small sugar bowl.

Bonds

SHORTLY AFTER MY BIRTHDAY Dad arrived by stagecoach. He shared my grief over Smokey and promised the pain I felt would be better by my next birthday. After you lose someone close, he told me, you think the pain will never go away. But he promised me that day by day, the hurt would ease a little as I learned to release it.

He asked if he should send Calico down, but I refused. It seemed disloyal to Smokey to replace him so soon. Dad understood my feelings.

Mother seemed glad to see Dad at first. As usual he had stories to make us laugh.

He told us Minniehaha was growing more stubborn every day. After Dad and Hud loaded her sides with sacks of ore, she refused to budge. He showed us with gestures how he had pushed her rear while Hud tugged at her lead but she'd planted her feet on the hill and swished her tail in Dad's face. "That pampered burro wanted her load lightened and that's what we finally had to do."

Sitting close beside him on the sofa beneath the bay window, I breathed in the smell of him; a dusty smell of tobacco and love.

Later that night, I was coming down stairs to tell my parents good night, when I heard their voices in our dining room. I paused on the stair for I never recovered from feeling a chill of horror on entering that room.

"That was a terrible place to raise a child, Elmer," I heard Mom say. "At least, I think she's lost that peculiar habit since I took her away from there."

She was talking about The Wad. Dad didn't answer. But after I was in bed, he came to sit beside me. He read a Kipling story about Ricky Ticky Tavy, a mongooose. In a whisper, he asked about my stories. Had I written any down?

I was still thinking about "my peculiar habit" and didn't want to talk about stories. I shook my head.

"You aren't happy here?"

I burst into tears. "It's awful."

He held my hand and told me he'd taken a lot of gold out of the mines. Now he must find a way to get it down to the assessor's office. Soon we would have enough money so we could all be together.

"But where?" I asked. That had always been the question.

Dad said when we struck it rich we'd spend the summers in the mountains and the winters in California.

I had been hearing those words for a long time. I knew Dad believed he would strike it rich one day. But I knew, too, that Mother had run out of patience.

Later I awoke to hear cross voices. Dad was trying to persuade Mom to come back with him. He said he hated to see her work so hard. She cried out that she worked just as hard for him and never got anything for it.

"I'm never going back there," she cried. "Never! Shirley hates it here after—after what happened to Smokey. I'll get her back to California and a decent life, if I have to steal to do it!"

I remembered the time Mom broke into the Robinson boy's house and I knew she meant it. What did she intend to do? Shivering, I pulled the covers up to my ears. It was a long time before I went to sleep. My dreams were troubled.

But the next morning the threat had moved away. It seems easier for me to recall the rare times my parents seemed happy together. Now I can almost hear their voices over breakfast in the tiny kitchen. Mother's cheeks flushed to their prettiest as she told Dad about the popular movie, *Patria*, that we'd seen the previous week.

She explained that it was a propaganda film that starred Irene Castle, America's darling. When I asked what a propaganda film was, Dad said it was a movie to sell people on the idea of going to war.

I was surprised that film companies could make movies like *Patria* if they weren't true. I tried to explain to Dad what a scary movie it was because it showed the awful things that could happen to people if they didn't prepare for war.

Dad snorted with disgust and said it was no doubt sponsored by the munitions companies.

It was a familiar subject. People, he believed, would always be manipulated by newspapers and movies. He said he could see our boys marching off to Wilson's war to become cannon fodder.

I was taking every word in with great interest. Most of the children at school had said *Patria* was a wonderful picture, and Mrs. Little had felt prompted to hang out her flag. I guessed they were being—manipulated.

I listened happily over my canned fruit. Almost I was their child that morning. War was one subject that Mother and Dad agreed upon. While they talked war, we had peace.

Two subjects made Dad pound his fist and raise his voice. One was religion. The other, war. Dad, a free thinker, turned avid at what he called brainwashing the masses. When I asked him about God, he said, "I can't believe he appointed any ambassadors down here, Turk. It's my belief that if He has any instructions for me, He'll let me know first hand."

I wondered that morning if God would let us know if we were meant to leave Dad and go to California.

Dad had cooked breakfast, and I smiled up at him while he helped us to scrambled eggs.

Mom continued to talk about the rash of propaganda films that had played Elko in the past months. When she mentioned *The Fall of the Nation*, I broke in and tried to help explain the plot. It had to do with a conspiracy against the republic. The defense bill was defeated in Congress because of a "friend of peace," who was shown to be the villain. He would be responsible for our enslaved nation.

I wanted to know if it was "good" to have peace, how could they make movies that told lies?

Dad gave me a long lecture on not believing everything I read or saw in the films. He repeated that there were always two sides, but what the country needed was someone brave enough to get up and state the unpopular cause: in this case, peace.

I kept thinking about what Dad said, and that's what got me into all the trouble. What is needed, he stated, was someone brave enough to take a stand against war.

That breakfast scene was implanted deeply in my mind. Wrapped in the joy of the three of us sharing an hour's happiness, I continued to think of the conversation. It was to have repercussions.

All of Elko Grammar School was to take part in the second Liberty Bond Drive. The teacher told us that it would have been better to have lost the War of Independence than to become a German slave. I didn't understand what she meant, except I knew she didn't agree with my parents. We were to write a composition about patriotism and the war effort.

Puzzled over what to write I remembered what Dad had said: someone should be brave enough to tell the other side.

That was what I decided to do. Mother kept my composition to show her family. Here, with corrected spelling, is what I wrote:

> *Patriotism is a bad disease that makes people want to kill*
> *one another. When governments want war they trick the*
> *people into wanting it, too. They make pictures such as*
> Patria *and* Fall of the Nation.

I wasn't certain how to go on from there until I came across a newspaper column. One maverick editor for the Elko paper was running editorials for peace and quoted Erasmus. I was looking for my "Little Nemo" cartoon, when I stumbled on these words. Delighted to find that "brave someone" who agreed with my parents, I labored countless hours to copy the editorial. My composition, with the Erasmus quote, would show the other side, I decided, and be different than the rest. I felt sure I'd get a gold star.

And, different it was. Here are Erasmus's words—words unlikely to inspire the sale of Liberty Bonds:

> "War, a festering sore, has broken out on the body of civilization . . . Let us not be deceived by a false sense of honor . . . Men are more terrible in the field of battle than ferocious beasts. The beast uses only the instinct and weapons that nature has supplied. Man uses the power of intellect, combined with weapons that would make the devil blush with shame . . ."

The day our school principal sat on the stage waiting to read the essays aloud was a big day for Elko. The school band played the "Star Spangled Banner." The large audience of families stood to salute the flag. The reverend from the Presbyterian Church led the school in prayer with the assurance that God was on our side against the terrible Huns.

Apparently the teacher had not had time or inclination to screen the essays before turning them over to the principal. One by one, he read compositions, all in the same vein of patriotism, all drawing a roar of applause. Then, he read mine.

He stopped at one point, frowned as if uncertain whether to continue, then with a puzzled frown, proceeded.

Silence ruled the auditorium when he finished. Then, there was a small pocket of insistent applause. It must have come from my parents. A babble of whispers followed. I felt all eyes focus on me in the front row. One kid stood and pointed to me.

The boy beside me asked, "Are you a Hun or somethin'?"
"Shirley Pedlar, I want to see you after the ceremony." Miss
Cowan, my teacher, looked stricken and angry.

On the way out I was followed by a buzz of voices. "That's the
dumb kid who lives at the hospital," one girl said. "She don't
know nuthin'."

"Don't you love your country?"

I never answered. I couldn't. My throat was tight. My voice had
dried up. Why was everyone mad? Didn't anyone want to hear
the "brave other side"?

In the schoolroom where I was summoned, Miss Cowan
demanded to know where I got such ideas.

Miserable, I looked up into her plump, red face.

"Answer me."

"Erasmus," I whispered.

She appeared puzzled, then took me to the blackboard. I was
not to participate in the picnic or games that day. I was to stay
inside and write on the board: "I love my country. I'd fight for
my country." I was to write it until all the blackboards were filled.

I guessed I was having my brain washed. It was plain that both
Erasmus and I had failed composition. Worst of all the whole
school knew I was—different. When I remembered Mom's word,
"peculiar," the tears started.

My parents tried to console me.

Mom said it was best to keep private conversation in the family. People who love their country most, she explained, criticize it
so it will be even better. "But many people don't understand that
and it won't make you popular to speak out."

"Poppycock!" Dad exploded. "I'm proud of the Turk for
expressing the truth. Your composition was wonderful, honey. I
want a copy to keep."

I should have expected them to disagree. I felt Dad was right
about it being a good thing to express the truth, but I wasn't so
sure I could be that Brave Someone to do it.

During the week following the Liberty Bond Drive, something happened that reminded me of what Erasmus had said about war. This time the war was on rabbits.

The town of Lamoile, a suburb adjoining Elko, was said to be overrun with rabbits. For some time we'd been hearing of a meat shortage and citizens were urged to eat wild game, especially jack rabbits. It was considered patriotic to save the red meat for our soldier boys.

Rabbits were rounded up in a field in Lamoile. Men went in with clubs, surrounded them and then "whacked them to death." I couldn't believe the talk at school. This was my first experience with savage cruelty. To hear the boys talk, it had been an exciting game that ended with the hunters enjoying a picnic.

"My dad got seven of the critters," one boy bragged with a fierce glint of pleasure. "Wow, you should have heard 'em crack skulls."

And he laughed.

I began to get sick at my stomach.

Those boys painted a graphic description of the rabbits crowded up against the fences, hundreds of them, screeching with fear as the clubs came down in their midst.

War on rabbits, too. I remembered Erasmus's words: "The beast uses only the instinct and weapons that nature has supplied. Man uses the power of intellect, combined with weapons that would make the devil blush with shame . . ."

I thought of Bonnie and my other pet rabbits. But it was unfair! Nature had failed to supply them with either instinct or weapons to protect themselves. They expected only kindness and trusted you. The fields belonged to them. We were the enemy.

Another boy told how he helped his father by killing the injured ones. I knew then that there were people who liked to kill, who found wars exciting. I waited for the teacher to tell the boys how cruel they'd been, but she nodded and said they had done their bit; the meat would help the war effort. I could think of nothing all day except those rabbits. I kept feeling their terror and suffering. I was unable to eat lunch.

In the afternoon, Miss Cowan asked if I were ill, and when I nodded, she sent me home.

"I do hope it's not the flu. The epidemic is far from over."

When I came home, crying, Mom hugged me close. "Never mind," she said. "You'll never have to go back to that school. We'll be leaving here forever next week."

Instead of comforting me, Mom's words multiplied my sorrow. It was happening. My family was breaking up. I found Dad packing to leave for The Divide. But where had Mom gotten the money?

When Dad learned about the rabbit massacre, he held me in his lap while I sobbed. Some of my copious tears may have been over the shocking discovery of violence in human hearts.

"As your friend, Erasmus, said, Turk, no wild beast is as cruel as man to man. And, I might add, as man to beast. I fear there's a bit of old Beelzebub in all of us." Dad went on, "And in some men that monster rules the roost."

"Who is—Beelzebub?" I asked as Dad dried my tears on his large handkerchief with the familiar smell of tobacco and love.

"Hatred of living things. That's what the devil means."

I thought about this in bed that night. Oh, how I hated those men and boys who clubbed the rabbits and could laugh about it! I hated and hated until I trembled with anger. I longed to gather the killers in a field and, when they were helpless, swing a club at them again and again. That night I recognized that Beelzebub must be in me, too.

Back to California

ONCE AGAIN WE are on a train. I look out the window at endless flatland dotted with sage. At Mother's suggestion, I sit with my legs doubled under me.

"If the conductor asks how old you are, you must say six and a half, do you understand?"

Why was Mother asking me to lie? Once she had spanked me for lying.

I ask her.

She says that we could only afford one ticket to California. If you were under seven you could ride free.

"But that's a lie." I protest. "I'm eight!"

She sighs and twists her mouth down in one corner; a mannerism I noticed lately.

Just a little white lie, she explains, and adds that when you're poor as church mice you're forced to lie at times.

Poor as church mice. Whenever I think about being poor, I think about being different; they go together. You have to lie and cheat conductors.

At such times I see myself as Somebody. A ballerina. Famous. Rich, proud, and not forced to lie. I will take care of Mother and she need never be ashamed of me because of my long legs. Can ballerinas have long legs?

The conductor moves down the aisle. I squirm on the stiff green upholstered seat. He comes slowly, asking questions and punching tickets.

Waiting for him is like waiting for the clock on the schoolroom wall while it moves only in small jerks after long intervals.

Would the conductor believe I was six and a half instead of eight and three weeks? If he didn't believe would they stop the train and put us off?

Finally he stands beside me with ticket stubs in one hand and a lot of papers in the other.

"How old are you, little girl?"

I open my mouth and no sound comes. It always happens when I get scared.

"She's six and a half," Mother snaps. "Seven next September."

"Is that true?" he demands of me.

That small, pink lie nibbles at me like a hungry field mouse. No words come. I look at my hands in my lap, gulp and nod. He snorts and walks away.

※

Mother pleaded with me not to look so serious. She repeated again and again how wonderful things would be in California. She talked of elegant restaurants, of plays and of the cousins who would come to play with me.

I can see her now, her cheeks flushed with excitement, eyes glinting with flecks of gold like Dad's ore.

One of her dreams was coming true. But my dreams were different. I must have wondered about her other dream. How could we have a home when we had no money? I'm sure I worried about what would become of us. I was a worrier.

All day on that train I was afraid to stretch my legs. I felt crunched. I squirmed on the seat because I wanted to go to the toilet, but I didn't dare to unfold yards of legs.

I remember little of that day. The coach car must have had the usual noises over the sound of the coal stove crackling and the raucous gossip of the wheels—children whining and people moving up and down the aisle chattering like squirrels. The coach would smell of coffee and garlic sausages and cigarette smoke.

But I remember only looking out the window, a way to avoid the present and what was happening. Mile after mile of prairie land was being snatched away. Each mile took me farther from my Dad, from The Divide, from home—and from that part of myself left behind. Later I heard Mother tell my aunt how it troubled her the way I kept twisting around in the seat to look back, never forward. Maybe I was expecting to see the Something-Left-Behind racing after the train like a forgotten child. Or a small black cat.

Smokey must have been on my mind that day for always, in lonely moments, I felt his warm, furry self pressed against my chest.

There was something even more painful on my mind. Dad had left for The Divide three days previous to our departure. Why hadn't he waited to say goodbye?

We were returning to Mother's family at the peach ranch in Selma where we had left when I was five. "Only temporary," Mother said. "Soon we'll have a home of our own."

I had heard these words so often from both parents that I must have looked skeptical. Trying to convince me, Mother explained about the terrible influenza epidemic spreading in California. Nurses were badly needed. Now she would have a job with good money. It would not take long to save enough for a payment on a home near her family in Oakland or Berkeley.

"You should know by now. Once my mind's been made up . . ."

Then she gave me a handkerchief and told me with some impatience to wipe my tears. She opened her purse and took out a letter. She had been keeping this, she said, until the conductor business was over.

When I recognized Dad's elegant handwriting, my heart must have made a ballet leap. The letter was addressed to Turk Pedlar. I knew I would keep it always.

> *Dear Little Turk,*
>
> *Do you perchance remember the little jug where we kept the liquid gold? I had harbored fervent hopes that there might be ample wealth within that magical receptacle to purchase another ticket to California. Alas, the gods of fortune did not smile. Why didn't I linger to say goodbye? Me believes you share my conviction that goodbyes are useless ceremonies with no purpose beyond inviting water to the eyeball. Ample dampness collects in that region without further contribution.*
>
> *So the little jug will grow heavier. In a few months you may expect my arrival in California and with this Aladdin vessel we shall purchase a domicile—small but with Noah Ark capabilities—a shelter to hold all the cats, dogs, turtles, frogs, and such creatures belonging to our social rank.*
>
> *Don't despair. I have told you this before. But now my promise splashes in the little jug.*
>
> *Maybe during the summer when school is recessed, you and I can return to The Divide to visit our many friends. Every time I step outside the cabin door, a squirrel or a robin reminds me of you. Take care of Mom and be cheerful.*
>
> *Love,*
> *Dad*

I sat there reading and re-reading his letter for most of the day before Mother said it was time to gather our things.

She stacked up sandwich wrappings, soiled napkins, and empty root beer bottles for the porter to take away. Then she opened the suitcase to put our books, my doll, her train slippers, and a box of fig newton cookies inside. It may have been the movements of her competent fingers that started me believing. I remembered her familiar words: "Once my mind is made up, you know how I am."

Her mind was made up when we moved to Tuscarora, then to Elko . . . and now to California. Each time she had worked and saved to make her dream possible. I could no longer doubt that she would have a house in California.

In every way my parents were different. While Mother worked and skimped and saved, Dad only worked, then left his dreams to a bit of magic. Maybe both ways brought results.

But Dad wasn't merely dreaming as usual. He wanted his family together. He was saving for a home. The little jug of liquid gold . . .

Maybe . . . just maybe, this time it could happen.

Selma, California
June 1918

Mom pointed out her family to me from the train window. I could see she was excited but all I wanted to do was turn the train around and return to the old mining camp in northeastern Nevada and my Dad.

Then the porter was helping me down onto the high step and into a rush of smelly steam from the engine.

"Tessie," someone's voice called, and then a woman rushed forward and caught Mom in a hug.

As sad as I felt over leaving Dad and being here in California, I had to feel a teeny bit glad for my mom. She had wanted above everything to return to California for as long as I could remember. Now she and her sister Agnes were hugging and crying on the platform under the dim light on the station.

"I can't believe we're really here," Mom said.

My Uncle Warren, a thin man with a playful smile behind his rogue's mustache, held my young cousin in his arms. Patricia's straight, blonde hair hung over his arm while she slept.

I'd always thought of my Mom as pretty, but she was outmatched by her sister's beauty. Both had the same heavy, brown hair with auburn lights, but Agnes wore hers in twists and curls on top of her head, while Mom had plain braids in what she called a coronet. Next to Agnes, full breasted and with round dimpled cheeks, my poor mother was far too thin. And her deep-set hazel eyes appeared lifeless next to Agnes's blue eyes, which danced with mischief.

Warren led us with pride to their 1916 Ford touring car. I can't say I enjoyed my first automobile ride. I sat in front with my uncle so Mother and her sister could talk in the back seat. When I climbed in, it felt something like sitting up on the high buckboard. But after Uncle Warren turned on the motor and we started chugging along the road at what seemed a reckless speed, I wanted to cry out to him to slow down.

"What do you think of it?" My uncle shouted to me.

"It's awfully stinky, isn't it?"

I didn't understand why the grown-ups found that funny.

"Surely you don't prefer the smell of horse manure?"

I must have nodded in my solemn way. Being accustomed to the smell of horses, I'd never considered animal excrement unpleasant. Remembering that smell made me nostalgic for Dolly and for home.

The Ford was awfully noisy. Along with the roar of the motor, wind whooshed and thundered while it clattered the isinglass curtains. I found the ride terrifying.

Talk and laughter from the back seat was somewhat reassuring. Long association with adults had inured me to eavesdropping. But I could catch no more than a few phrases over the racket. Something about new industry in California. "Tess, you won't believe the changes since the motorcar has become so popular," Agnes said.

Mother, as she told me later, found the changes in California since she'd been gone astonishing. My uncle said the population of the state had nearly doubled in the last ten years while there had been phenomenal expansion of new industry.

As startling as this may have seemed to residents, it was unbelievable to Mother. She had left California when wagons and buckboards still occupied country roads, when plows were horse and mule driven. She remembered church socials and evenings at home playing cards or gathering around the piano for group singing. Now there were drives into town and movie houses—more than one to choose from. A new society and culture, hitched to the automobile, brought trucks, tractors, and rapid communication. Agnes and Warren spoke of unrestricted travel, jitney buses (slang for a small bus that carried passengers for five cents), filling stations, garages, hot-dog stands, paved highways, parking lots, and traffic citations. A new language to my bewildered mother.

Both my aunt and uncle were jolly people. Apparently they were very much in love, for Warren shook with silent laughter at everything Agnes said or did. And Agnes refused to take anything seriously. She'd been one of the daring turn-of-the-century girls, bold enough to dance on a cabaret table at San Francisco's Coffee Dan's one New Year's Eve. In 1906 she'd lost all she owned in the San Francisco earthquake. Then her first marriage to a well-off captain on a maritime vessel ended. A few years later she met and fell in love with a saloon keeper, Warren Wells.

Married five years, they had scraped together enough capital to buy a mortgage on a peach ranch in Selma, where Patricia, now four, was born. Agnes was one of the most jolly people I had ever known. And I, whom everyone said was "such a serious little girl," longed to be just like my aunt.

One night I was reading in the big farm kitchen where the family assembled. The parlor was reserved for company.

I overheard my mother tell my aunt, "The trouble with Elmer is he has no ambition."

Agnes was washing dinner dishes, Mother wiping them.

"That's bad," Agnes said. "Like a car with a dead battery."

She chuckled at her own joke and Uncle Warren put down his paper to shake with silent laughter.

But that wasn't true. Dad worked hard digging and hauling ore while he dreamed of striking gold. I wasn't certain what "ambition" meant. I guessed it meant to want something better than living in a mountain cabin. But I felt sure there couldn't be anything better.

However, during those first few weeks on my relatives' ranch, in spite of missing my Dad, I was happier than I'd been in a long time. I was too young to know why. Now I'm certain it was space and solitude. I had missed the silence of The Divide. Out in the vineyards of the peach ranch there were no people to absorb space and it was like being set free again after long captivity.

Besides the orchards, Warren had planted the few acres in grapes and that was where I found this favorite retreat. The ground was warm on my bottom. I liked the smell of earth and vines of decaying fruit while friendly flies and bees buzzed around me. Once again I could create a satisfying world. I am not certain what stories I told at that time. It could have been an adventure of Heidi or Nadine on a peach ranch. Or, perhaps, I summoned my great mechanical elephant and journeyed back to The Divide or Bull Run.

The house with its two stories was larger than any I'd ever lived in. An old ranch house with a tower and windmill, it was set back behind several acres of peach trees. Selma is "the home of the peach," as a highway sign informs travelers.

One day when I returned to the house after happy hours in the vineyard, Mother's face puckered into a worried scowl as she looked at the front of my skirt. I turned away smoothing out the wrinkles left by The Wad. I waited for her to reprimand me but she said nothing. Her silence made it worse. I guessed my behavior was unspeakable.

But later that day I made a discovery about the ranch that helped me forget Mother's disapproval—cats and kittens. A plethora of them! I chose a white one and called it Snowball. Soon that furry personality was at my heels wherever I went. I had missed Smokey every day and secretly grieved for him. Snowball helped heal the wound.

My main annoyance turned out to be my cousin Patty. Four years younger than me, she, like Snowball, wanted to shadow me. I hid in the vineyards to escape her and felt guilt when I heard a small forlorn voice calling my name.

Other voices intruded on my imagination that summer. Agnes

and Warren were concerned over the big ranches with out-of-state owners who were making major decisions at the Grange, an organization of farmers. Two subjects, besides the Grange, dominated the dinner table; one was the military versus the pacifist viewpoint on the war; the other with equally opposing views was closed- or open-shop policies of the unions. Warren and Agnes did not believe we should be pushed into a "foreign war," nor did they believe ranchers should be forced to adopt the closed-shop policy of unions.

The state's agricultural development, accelerated by the war, brought such new industries as meat packing, the canning of fruit and vegetables, and the processing of other important foods. While most of the earlier industries, such as petroleum, lumber, and motion pictures, were California owned and operated, many new enterprises represented the westward expansion of eastern corporations.

Mother needed a job. I overheard her tell my aunt that Dad had sent her no money. "Not that I really expected it," she added with bitterness.

The job was supplied by California Fruit Growers Supply Company. By acquiring large holdings of timber land in northern California and by operating its own mills, this organization was able to supply box material to the growers at a reasonable cost. So now the ranchers hired not only pickers but packers. Over Agnes's protest that her sister didn't need to work, my independent mother insisted on trying her hand at packing peaches.

As this operation took place on the ranch, Mother felt she could keep an eye on me and earn, eventually, enough to make a payment on a home for the two of us.

It was because of Patty, my troublesome cousin, that I joined the peach packers that summer.

The cats and kittens were enjoying a pan of milk on the back porch, when I swooped up the white one.

Immediately Patty wanted that cat.

"Give it to me. It's mine."

"Get another one," I told her. "Snowball's mine."

Mother spoke from the breakfast table. "Give it to her. She's only four. You're a big girl."

I failed to see the logic. Why should being younger entitle you to privileges? When I wanted something it worked the other way—then I was told, "You're not old enough."

I gave Patty the cat and stuck my tongue out at her.

Maybe it was because of that. Maybe it was curiosity that made her do it. She walked into the kitchen and stuck Snowball's paw against the big iron stove. Snowball screeched an indignant howl and leaped down, leaving scratches on the culprit's arm. At the same time, I snatched Patty's hand and stuck it against the stove.

Of course the little brat screamed and bawled. Her fingers were only slightly red.

Instantly Mother and Agnes jumped up from the table. Agnes hurried Patty off to the bathroom for treatment. Mother's fingers dug into my shoulder and she marched me off to the bedroom for treatment of a different kind. It was the only time she ever spanked me with a hair brush. I cried and hiccuped at the injustice of it all. Mother explained the problem of being poor and dependent.

"This is not your home. Remember that. You are a guest here. You make it very hard on me when you forget it."

Someday, someday, said the small voice that had been talking to me lately, you'll be somebody. You'll own a better home than this one and you'll be rich and never, never have to be a guest again. Could Mother really believe it was better being a guest here than living in our own cabin? That night I cried many homesick tears for that cabin and for Dad.

I resolved to practice dancing every day. I'd be a ballerina while I was young, later I'd write stories. But instead of the ethereal life of a ballerina, I embarked the next day on the lowly career of a peach packer. For the next morning, Mother insisted I go to work with her.

"Oh Tessie, don't take life so seriously," Agnes pleaded. "Patty wasn't hurt. Likely she learned a good lesson. Leave the youngster here."

Mother, always the worrier, was adamant.

So, daily I went to the long table out near the road and for a time helped to pack the fuzzy peaches into wooden boxes. Mother's hands worked faster than anyone's at that table. Mine fumbled as if fingers were missing. Quickly I grew bored and my arms ached from reaching.

The foreman, a stout woman, walked between the tables, observing us. Sometimes she complained that the fruit was packed too closely, other times, not close enough.

We were the only white packers, the rest were Mexicans. Some of the packers lived in tents on the ranch; others camped out under the trees. Mother told me we received ten cents for every box that passed inspection. The average packer made from fifty to seventy cents a day. Mother made a dollar or more and a lot of enemies at the table.

When I left the table to move closer to the other children, wanting to join in their games, their mothers called to them.

"Why don't they want their children to play with me?" I asked Mother.

"Because we're relatives of the ranchers, honey," she explained. "They resent us for not being one of them."

Many of the ranchers, including my aunt and uncle, were conservative Republicans, struggling to pay off mortgages, to battle bugs and disease among the crops and to worry about over-production, weather conditions, and falling prices. Most ranchers were naively unaware of the workers who picked and packed their crops. Some growers were willfully callous concerning the simple rights and decencies of life they denied the migrants. Long-established custom was to take for granted the exploitation of the laborer.

So four years earlier, the Industrial Workers of the World came to inspect the Wheatland Ranch, where there were only four toilets (none for women), where there was no drinking water in the fields where the temperature rose to 104 and beyond, where the nearest grocery was a concession provided by relatives of the rancher.

Labor leaders, taking advantage of a mass meeting that had been called to protest these conditions, worked the crowd at Wheatland up to an explosive stage. When the sheriff and deputies arrived to quell the riot, two of the workers, one a young boy, was shot. Many others suffered injuries.

The state established a Commission of Immigration and Housing with authority to inspect labor camps. Definite improvement was made for comfort, decency, and sanitation. But many of the problems were far too complicated to solve by legislation alone.

Agnes and Warren provided adequate toilets for both men and women; pitchers of ice water were kept on a table. However, neither pickers nor packers received a living wage. Wages were decided by the Grange and the ranchers were bound to stick together—a privilege denied the workers. Most ranchers, my relatives included, fought against the closed-shop policy needed by the unions to keep strike breakers from taking jobs.

One night I heard conversation at dinner about my fellow workers that puzzled me. It must have gone something like this:

"I'm afraid we've got some of those damned Wobblies among the packers," my uncle said as he cut up Patty's meat.

"What are—Wobblies?" I asked.

"It's an expression," my aunt explained, "for a Bolshevik organization. They are dangerous because they want to change our government."

I straightened up in my chair. It wasn't the first time I'd heard about Bolsheviks. I'd even been called one. But how could these peach packers be dangerous?

"Some of the packers at the Grange are worried," Warren said. "Since the Mooney affair, union leaders have become damn powerful."

Later I learned that Mooney, a prominent labor leader, with his partner, Billings, were sent to jail following a bombing in a San

Francisco Labor Day parade. Recently, my uncle explained, the two men had been acquitted of the charges. But the martyrdom of Mooney and his friend proved a big boost to the unions and their closed-door policy.

"Uprisings and riots," my uncle concluded, "are becoming too frequent for comfort."

I understood enough of this conversation to gather it was risky to pack peaches.

A few days later, during lunch hour, the migrant workers gathered in knots, talking in low voices. Then a young man climbed up on the table, said a few rapid words in Spanish and people began to sing.

"It's one of the I.W.W. songs," my Mother whispered, drawing back and looking frightened. "They're getting ready for trouble."

Voices rose in anger. Some of the men carried pipes and their faces looked mean and menacing. I moved closer to Mother who was standing near the bench.

"Run," she whispered. "Run back to the ranch as fast as you can and warn Agnes to call the sheriff."

She picked up her handbag and without waiting to see more, I darted off. More angry shouts in Spanish broke out.

"Hurry!" Mom called from behind me. She was running, too.

When I saw the two men with pipes running after us, I screamed. Maybe that was why they dropped back. Maybe they only wanted to frighten us away. It is likely they resented Mother taking a job from another migrant worker.

The sheriff and posse arrived in time to quiet the crowd without a riot. But Mother decided it was too dangerous to work any longer as a peach packer. I shudder to think what could have happened to us, being relatives of despised ranchers.

Mother had a chance to take a job as a saleswoman in a dry goods store in Selma, but I was the problem.

It must have been a great relief to her when her sister Kitty arrived from Berkeley with her husband, Will, and daughter, Helen. The Dunnings offered a solution to Mom's problem.

Berkeley
Summer 1918

THE DAY MY Berkeley relatives arrived at the peach ranch, I decided they must be awfully rich. They drove up in a car such as I'd never seen. Long, black, sleek, and shiny, it didn't chug and rattle like Uncle Warren's Ford. Instead, Uncle Will's car purred like a chorus of contented cats and smelled like new leather inside. Two extra chairs, called jump seats, unfolded between the front and back seats.

Later I learned the car was called the Will King. I associated the name with my uncle Will Dunning, who played a kingly role. He wore gold-rimmed glasses and strongly resembled Woodrow Wilson. Will was a dental technician in Berkeley, and his overly white and slightly bucked front teeth flashed like an advertisement for his business.

My aunt, Mother's sister Katherine, was called "Kitty" and it suited her. Frail in appearance with gentle manners, Kitty spoke in a thin voice that coaxed and consoled. When Will shouted or Helen sulked, Aunt Kitty would say, "Now Will . . ." Or, "Now Helen . . ." My aunt could make "now" into the most soothing word in the language. Content to sit quietly by Will's side, she gazed at him, pale blue eyes aglow with adoration.

"Will's not easy to live with," Aunt Agnes told Mother. "I'm amused at the way Kitty caters to him. I could never live like that, but she seems happy, doesn't she?"

In between soothing Will's rooster feathers, Aunt Kitty tried to cajole a smile from my sulky cousin. Helen, two years my junior, was a thin child with straight fair hair. Her one claim to beauty—brown eyes that were large and distinctive against the pallor of her cheeks—was flawed. An optometrist told the family that Helen would be blind within five years. If I'd ever heard what the disease was, I have forgotten. After seeing many specialists, Kitty and Will turned to Christian Science and constantly affirmed that their child would not lose her sight.

I can see her now as she looked the day they arrived at the ranch, wearing a white cotton dress with a low waistline where her hips might someday be. A large pink hair bow in a gold clip clung precariously to a few thin strands of light hair. She tugged constantly at her mother's skirts and whined.

Being two lonely children drawn to each other, yet extremely shy, we found this first confrontation frightening. We amused the grown-ups by circling around the dining room table while each kept a wary eye on the other. Agnes suggested I show Helen the vineyard. No response. The windmill tower? We continued to stalk each other until Agnes's voice boomed out, "The kittens!" And that did it.

The following week, Helen left her mother's skirts to follow me like a heel-trained pup. That week I found an audience, other than myself, to listen to a story. The story I told was about a lost child, Sarah, trying to find her way home. I believe I remember parts of this story because, at Helen's request to hear more, I made Sarah's story into a serial. Around that time I must have grown self conscious about The Wad, for I remember bunching a handkerchief into a ball, then concealing it within my hands, which I clasped in my lap and moved to the rhythm of a rising excitement. Helen never participated in my tales. Neither did she interrupt. She sat, passive, lips parted, brown eyes curious, intent and appealing.

"Do let her come home with us for a visit, Tess?" Aunt Kitty pleaded. "They'll be good company for each other."

My sense of adventure urged me to go while the long habit of dependence bound me to Mother.

"It will only be for a short time, darling," Mother urged, "and so exciting for you to live in the city."

"Can I take Snowball?" I asked. This was blackmail for I knew the grown-ups wanted me to go. After some hesitation, everyone agreed.

My mother's family, I soon discovered, developed a hierarchy all its own. The brothers-in-law, all so different, had become—likely from constant association—as close as the sisters. The McDonald Clan, as Dad referred to them, never needed outsiders. When they were together, the men played poker in the evenings. Usually Agnes played with them. The other sisters gathered to sew and talk about ways to save on coal, and help the war effort by cooking with less sugar and how they disliked the strange, dark breads. Opinions clashed yet never appeared to mar the shared affection.

Uncle Warren and Uncle Will Dunning differed as much as two men could. Warren came in from the vineyard in his blue coveralls, smelling like earth and fertilizer.

His speech and manner suggested he had seen enough of life to find it all somewhat amusing, and good humor lines around his mouth deepened when he spoke. He talked in the leisurely manner of a bartender ready to relax and listen to customers. His words, often raunchy, were never mean, seldom heated.

Will Dunning, straight and thin, wearing his gray or brown business suit, shoes polished (by Kitty), would rise to offer a hand to his back-slapping brother-in-law. The aunts said Will had been a "dandy" in his youth. Yet well-dressed as he always was, Uncle Will failed to look dapper. He never appeared relaxed in his clothes as Dad did—even in B.V.D.'s. From beneath a dictatorial manner, a gauche farm boy—with those slightly bucked teeth—would re-appear unexpectedly. But, as a child, I was awed by what I considered to be my uncle's sophisticated city manners.

Will's English was slangy. Lacking my father's extensive vocabulary, he spoke in the same quick and jerky manner that he drove the car, seldom using gestures. He was always on the move, and I can hear him say to Aunt Kitty, "Let's get on the road, kid." Or "Let's get goin', so we can get back."

Will was sympathetic with Warren's concern over the big land-owners from the east swallowing up all "the little guys."

"Still," he argued, "got to be grateful for big corporations. They provide jobs for the little guys."

"Hell, Will, they keep the little guy under thumb. Something's happening in our country right now, and God damn it, if it's not stopped—"

About this time Aunt Kitty would venture into the argument. "Now Will, don't be upset."

But it was Aunt Agnes's hearty voice that put an end to conflict. "Turn it off, boys. Turn it off. Let's play poker."

The day came when I told Mother goodbye and climbed into one of the small jump seats of the Will King car to motor west. Snowball meowed in his box by my feet. When Mom kissed me she whispered, "Don't forget you're a guest in their home." Her words reminded me that I had no home. My dad was far away in the mountains and now I was losing my mother. In tearful panic, I tried to tell Mom I didn't want to go. But we were gliding down the drive, for my uncle never wasted time in getting underway.

The time we made in Uncle Will's car on this trip became one of his favorite topics of conversation.

"Moved right along we did. Got her up to 25 miles an hour on those valley roads. Came down from Selma in ten hours, even with stops . . ."

Will grumbled over those gas-stops.

"Now hurry, girls," Kitty urged nervously.

And Will held a stopwatch on us every time we beelined for a toilet.

Mother's "short time" stretched and, from mid-June until the end of July, I lived with the Dunnings in a flat above the U.C.

Theater on Berkeley's University Avenue. Will's Dental Laboratories occupied the floor below the flat. A grocery next door shared the rear yard, which was partly covered to protect the boxes of produce in those days before refrigeration. Here Helen, Snowball, and I played. I missed the sensation of space and the large view of sky.

It was a life far removed from my shanty above Tuscarora. While I continued to long for that home and Dad, slowly I discovered the pleasures Mother found in city life.

Those who could afford it enjoyed the many fine restaurants and theaters San Francisco offered.

With the novelty of moving pictures fading, theater managers turned back to vaudeville in various forms; some advertised "live" prologues before the movie, while stage shows gained in popularity.

Friday night was kid's night. Uncle Will said so. That he was one of the "kids" I never guessed until later.

"Get your duds on, kids. We're going to the show."

The show might mean the Jack Russell "girly show," playing at Oakland's Century Theater, or the more elaborate and sophisticated Fanchon and Marco Revue, playing in San Francisco.

This was our favorite, partly because it meant a trip across the bay on the auto ferry. Aunt Kitty taught us the popular songs and we would stand near the rail of the ferry, gazing out at the moon reflected on the bay and sing, "Two Little Girls In Blue, Lad"; "Over There"; "Yankee Doodle"; a scrubbed-up version of "Hinky Dinky Parlez Vous," and duets of "Oh, Mr. Gallagher, Oh, Mr. Sheen." As our thin voices went out over the water, I discovered that Helen's voice was the musical one.

> *There's a silver lining*
> *Through the dark clouds shin-ing . . .*

But I didn't need a musical voice to become a dancer or a writer. No doubt it was my uncle's reverence for stage shows that stimulated my ambition to be a dancer. Will subscribed to show magazines (as well as the raunchy *Whiz Bang*) so he knew the names of most of the Ziegfeld cast as well as those of local performers.

One night, on the ferry, we gazed back at the sprinkle of lights on the Oakland and Berkeley hills. Uncle Will pointed out a gray battleship with cannons pointed toward us. Quickly I turned away. Instead I sought enchantment in the smell of salt water, of freshly ground coffee, and chocolate in the air as we glided closer and closer to the exciting city. Screeching gulls followed in our wake, and the Ferry Building with all its lights, the tallest building towering over its city, was always "The Fairy Building" to me.

We heard the gentle splash of paddle wheels in the dark, then the grinding noise of engines as the ferry boat, nearing the pier, went into reverse. A well-lit billboard of a man in golden robes, who could be Arab or Moroccan, lifted his coffee cup to drink to us.

Even the Casino Theater was an innovation. Instead of the usual 600 seats, this theater boasted a thousand upholstered chairs. For show business, as the nation sought relief from war jitters, 1918 was a booming year.

"Big theaters are the fad," Uncle Will said, explaining that New York had recently opened a theater that seated five thousand.

It was not unusual to see the dancers, in abbreviated costumes, circulating through the house selling Liberty Bonds. Newspapers and newsreels ran daily editorials to keep the public aware of German subs sinking our ocean liners. After kidding with the pretty dancer, Uncle Will bought a bond to prove his patriotism.

The show staged by Fanchon and Marco in daring costumes caught my imagination—a visual, make-believe story! Helen and I sat in the front row chewing taffy from our Prize Packages and gazing up at the wonderful dancers. I longed to be able to dance my stories.

When I told Helen this, she said, "I'll tell my mother we want dancing lessons if you like."

I couldn't believe this would really happen, but it did. Helen's every wish was granted. The next week we were enrolled in The Johnson School of Classical and Skirt Dancing for Young Misses.

Poor Helen lacked the necessary energy, and before the *barre* work was finished, so was she. The sensation of moving to music captivated me; even the simple *pliés*—bending of knees to a squatting position—and *relevés*—rising on toe. The phonograph scratched through "Kiss in the Dark."

Headed for trouble, I practiced spins and kicks with no regard for place or space.

"She's overly ambitious," I overheard Aunt Kitty tell her sister Aunt Ann Williford. "Like Tessie."

Aunt Williford, as Helen and I called her, apparently had the taste for elegant clothes. I supposed that was why she'd chosen those fancy dresses from the City Of Paris store for me.

"She's not at all like Tessie," Aunt Williford replied to Kitty in her sharp tone. "She's just like Elmer Pedlar. She's got his easygoing disposition and storytelling ability."

Who was I like? Which parent did I hope to follow? Energy bubbled in me ready to spill over. It drove me to respond in some physical way. I was determined to master *pirouettes*.

The wonderful surge of energy occurred while my aunt purchased sliced ham in a Berkeley delicatessen. Helen leaned against her mother, teasing for cookies.

I spun on one toe, swung out my foot for needed balance, then—crash—it happened. My foot went through the glass on the ice chest that held sliced meat and salads. Built like a horizontal box about six feet wide, the ice box had a number of shelves for food above the blocks of ice. Now shattered glass covered shelves and floor.

I stood rooted in shock hiding my hot face in both hands. The store keeper spoke first and she kept right on speaking in a voice far from calm.

"She didn't mean to do it," Helen cried, in loyal defense. "She can't help it. She loves to dance."

I heard Aunt Kitty's timid voice arranging to pay for the damage. Guilt sentenced me to self-loathing. Not only had I caused my aunt expense and embarrassment but Mom would find out. She would insist on paying and she worked hard for every nickel. Why couldn't I have stayed in Nevada where there was space for whatever was in me that wanted out?

"Aren't we going to get lunch meat?" Helen asked, after my aunt paid the bill and we started to leave.

"We'll have peanut butter sandwiches," Kitty said. I knew she had to ask Will for household money. So he would know what I'd done. I would never be a good guest and I was so tired of trying. I wondered if my family would ever be together in our own home, or if I'd be a guest for the rest of my life?

The scolding I expected never came. My aunt looked at me and said, "It's all right, honey. I'm sure you'll be more careful next time."

I never loved her more than I did at that moment. But about that time a growing loneliness began and I worried over both of my parents. What were they doing? Why didn't Mother come for me as she'd promised?

When I thought about my parents, I couldn't help but compare my parents' marriage with that of the Dunnings. The harmony between Will and Kitty kept their home as comfortable and warm as my old beaver-lined coat. I never heard my aunt raise her voice. But as much as I admired her, I wondered if, inside, she was feeling like her tightly wound sewing bobbin? That was the way I felt while I strained to please my uncle. Why did women have to please men all the time to keep peace?

Looking back now I believe the collective thinking of those war years left the female on the old pedestal, but slightly off balance. Popular songs portrayed the girls who lit up the dreams of service men away from home: "I want a girl, just like the girl, who married dear old dad." "My darling Nellie Grey," "Mother Macree." Many of the newer songs referred to sweethearts and wives as "my baby."

But the suffragettes suggested roles for women that bore little resemblance to those soft, pink girls painted by Mary Cassatt.

An increasing number of women worked outside the home. With husbands off at war, wives became heads of households. This was most confusing to my generation—we, who would become the wives of tomorrow. In newspapers we saw the suffragettes portrayed in ugly images—cartoons of large, masculine females in pants and boots.

A number of women working in munitions factories in England refused to wear pants: "We're women," they protested, "and we refuse to dress like men."

I didn't want to "wear the pants in the family" as people said. Neither did I want to be invisible like Kitty. I dreamed of a career. Maybe it would be better not to get married at all.

More than once that summer, a wave of desolation would sweep over me. At night, in bed, I would think of my mom and dad, and of the home of my own in the mountains. It was around that time that Helen's vision became too blurred for reading, and a Christian Science practitioner came to treat her. Along with Helen, I recited the Prayer of Faith.

> *God is my health, I can't be sick.*
> *God is my strength, unfailing quick.*
> *God is my all. I know no fear . . .*

I found the belief comforting at a time when my family was scattered.

Later when we were in our teens, Helen once asked me if I believed in Christian Science.

"Like all religions, I do and I don't," I replied. "I'm an agnostic like my Dad."

She appeared horrified. "How do you think we got here if God didn't make us?"

"Perhaps like gold gets inside the mountain." I tried to explain my belief that the mountain was made up of boulders, clay, sand, and debris—collected over the years, "something like the way we accumulated a lot of ancestors," I told my cousin.

Among this debris, I believed, may run a vein of gold. Through the ages, Dad once explained, rock and vein material get eroded and washed away with rain.

She laughed. "You mean maybe Grandfather McDonald was—eroded?"

I guessed we were all eroded but I liked to remember that gold was heavier than debris and remained in the pan.

"How do you get to be—gold—and not washed away?"

I tried to explain my belief in some mysterious force for good that constantly battles evil. "It's like music," I told my cousin, thinking of Dad. "If you can keep tuned and move to your inner music, you express the Good—that's God."

Dad wrote to us, and Mother enclosed parts of his letters with hers. Sometimes I wrote to my Dad but there seemed to be little in my life anymore that I felt would interest him. Perhaps I had a sense of disloyalty for my awakening interest in the entertainment offered by the city, especially theater.

I was thinking about this on the afternoon when Aunt Kitty told us she was planning a dinner party for Aunt Williford and Uncle Alfred.

"We want to celebrate their fifteenth anniversry. You must both promise me to act like little ladies that evening. You can come to the party if you'll sit still and not dance around and make Aunt Williford nervous. You know she's not used to children."

The warning was for me. I resolved to be as quiet and listless as my cousin when the Willifords came.

Ann Williford was always *Aunt* Williford to all the cousins. This was significant as we were taught to call all the other aunts by first names—Aunt Agnes, Mary, Bessie, Kitty, Ellie, Tessie, and— *Aunt* Williford.

She was slender, of medium height, and carried herself as if tightly corseted. Her personality, too, had a whalebone restraint. I believe she made a lonely life for herself by being one of those people whose quick tongues insult friends and relatives. I knew she loved her sisters' children—all of them. She had none of her own. She lavished gifts on us, handmade undergarments with embroidered initials and those regrettable dresses from City Of Paris. She invited us for dinners and overnight visits, took us to Lehnharts and Pig N' Whistle for ice cream and pastries. Then she ended the day with a few sharp words that spoiled it all.

I can hear the other aunts whispering, "Ann is in one of her moods. Be careful."

Oddly enough one way to annoy her was with a gift.

"I really do not need any more handkerchiefs." Her voice would be curt. "Why don't you keep them for yourself."

Her big house on Grove Street was always in perfect order. The sisters relied on Ann's good taste and admired her pretty clothes.

Alfred was a gentle man with a rotund figure and happy disposition. Aunt Agnes once remarked, "Who but Alfred could put up with Ann?"

Now they were coming to a dinner party and the Dunning flat bustled with plans: silver to polish, curtains to wash, shopping.

"I want to run up something to wear," Aunt Kitty told us one day. "Ann always looks so stylish."

A column of fashion articles by the dancer Fanchon appeared daily with pictures of her creations in the *Call Bulletin.* Kitty cut these out each week and put them in a scrap book.

One evening she showed a picture to Uncle Will.

"Isn't she talented, Will? Imagine being able to draw and design like this as well as write and dance?"

Will took the paper and glanced at Fanchon in a gown, slightly above the ankles with strange puckers on her slim hips, referred to as "bullet pockets, the latest style."

He nodded approval. "Now that's what I call looking snappy."

The next day Kitty took us shopping and she purchased the blue serge mentioned in the column. For the next couple of days she spent hours cutting and basting. Then a whirring, creaking noise filled the flat as Kitty's foot flew up and down on the pedal of her sewing machine. From time to time she tried the dress on, asked our opinion and had me pin up the hem as she turned slowly in front of a door mirror. The hemline was three inches above the ankle, not the daring six inches being shown.

The night before the dinner party, she put it on, touched her lips with pink rouge, and went into the living room. "Will?"

"Yeah?" He never looked up from reading the sports column about Dempsey's fight.

"I made a new dress for the party. What do you think?"

Will took off his thin, gold-rimmed glasses and gave Kitty a startled look. His lips parted, then he started to laugh.

"Great Scott kid, what kind of a rig is that?"

I looked away from my aunt's face, afraid she was going to cry.

"What's that bunched-up material on your hips for?" he asked.

"Those are the—bullet pockets," she whispered. "Will, it's—it's the dress you liked so much from 'Fanchon's Fancies.'"

Still chuckling, Will shook his head. "It's not right for you, kid. You're not the type. Fanchon could get by with anything."

I followed my aunt to the bedroom.

"I think it looks real nice on you, Aunt Kitty."

She bent and kissed me. "Thank you dear, but Will's perfectly right. I've wasted my money. I'll just wear the same old rose print he likes."

On the night of the dinner party, Aunt Williford and Uncle Alfred arrived with gifts for Helen and me. She brought us sewing sets, paper dolls, and candy. Then she hugged us and admired our ruffled, taffeta dresses made by Aunt Kitty. We followed her into the bedroom.

As Aunt Williford put her long tailored jacket on the bed, Aunt Kitty whispered, "I've something to show you." She took the dress with the bullet pockets from the closet and explained how she'd copied it from the newspaper column.

"Will doesn't think it suits me. So I—well, I thought that perhaps you might like to have it."

Aunt Williford stiffened. "I don't need your castoffs."

This time Aunt Kitty's pale blue eyes filled with tears. "Oh—oh, I didn't mean—"

I decided Aunt Williford was cruel.

"I can't imagine why you'd think I'd wear anything so, so—theatrical."

Silently Kitty hung the dress back in the closet and we returned to the living room.

Aunt Williford showed she regretted her behavior, even though she never apologized. "Kitty, your place looks so nice. Aren't those pillows new?" After a moment, she said sweetly, "Fanchon is clever, isn't she? I've read the columns, but Alfred and I haven't seen the show yet."

I guessed she hurt from feeling guilty and I was—almost—sorry for her.

During the evening my uncles talked about the war winding down. Will Dunning believed the country was in for some hard times with more than two million soldiers soon returning from overseas, needing jobs. The two men deplored the latest strikes and both agreed that the I.W.W. was the curse of the times.

My aunts talked mostly of the high cost of everything—rent, food, clothing. "Why milk has jumped from nine cents a quart to fifteen cents!"

While Helen and I played a card game, I listened with one ear. Aunt Williford asked Kitty if she thought the suffrage bill would pass. My Aunt Kitty didn't appear to know much about it. But Aunt Williford felt certain that women would run the country one day and do a much better job. "It's time and then some that we had our say!"

Will Dunning remarked that Warren might be selling his ranch to one of the big eastern corporations.

Helen said sadly, "I suppose if Uncle Warren sells his ranch, your mother will be coming to get you."

She was right.

Shortly after the anniversary party, Helen and I were in the U.C. Theater for the weekly children's matinee: Mary Pickford was playing in *Daddy Long Legs*. Al St. John, whose name we interpreted as Al Street John, was the comedy feature with a thrilling Pearl White serial.

Mother slipped in behind us and touched my shoulder.

"Hello darling," she whispered. Her presence snatched me back into security even before I was around the aisle and in her arms. In the warm touch of her skin, the special smell and the love given in her hug, I knew pure joy that day, a feeling I can neither describe nor forget.

"I'll never leave you again," she promised. "I've missed you so."

After those first glowing moments of reunion, I needed to know if she had come to get me. Did we have a home now?

"The Willifords have room and we'll be staying on in Berkeley with them for a while."

I muffled a sigh. I liked Aunt Williford but she did have a sharp tongue and little patience with children. I would miss Helen for I had learned to love her that summer. Having a cousin was almost as good, I decided, as having a sister.

"I'm going to get a job nursing," Mom said. "It won't be long, sweetheart, before you'll have your own home."

Mom had been saying that for a long time. I hoped she was right about getting a house, but I knew it would never be home until Dad returned.

What difficult years these must have been for Mom. It took great courage to nurse through the contagious influenza epidemic, but I'd never known my mother to be afraid. At times the dream of saving enough to buy a home for us must surely have seemed impossible. Yet she never gave up.

That night I wondered if we would always be the poor country mice visiting city relatives.

The Funeral Game

ONE MORNING AS I started down the stairs in Aunt Williford's home, I heard Mother talking in whispers.

"She's not to know," Mother said to my aunt. "I'm taking the day off. I'll take her to a picture show in San Francisco."

"She's bound to find out, Tessie. It's in all the papers."

I crouched on the stairs with my two dolls dressed in black for the day's funeral services. Frightened now, I wondered what I was not to know.

"We must keep it from her. She's too young to understand."

&

I was eight and five months that fall of 1918 and Mother and I had moved into the two-story house in Berkeley with the Willifords, and Mother's younger sister, Aunt Mary. I stayed with Aunt Williford while Mother worked as a practical nurse during the epidemic of Spanish influenza. Aunt Mary worked for a travelers' aid in the San Francisco Ferry Building. She was in her twenties. I adored my younger aunt, who took time to play games or to read to me in the evenings. She had a way of sharing glances with me to suggest that she and I were in alliance against the older generation. This usually happened when Aunt Williford made a sharp remark to either of us. Because of Aunt Mary's silent suggestion that we shrug off Aunt Williford's criticisms, I was less uncomfortable in that house than I would have been.

My aunt's house stood next door to the Burke Funeral Home, a brown-shingled building with window shades fringed in black. A gray car that my aunt called a hearse would glide down the driveway separating the two houses. This meant nothing to me, for anything connected with death was a mystery.

My first awareness of death had occurred near the entrance of Tuscarora, where the old cemetery sprawled down the hill. The overgrowth of gray sagebrush cast soft shadows, partly concealing stone markers, wooden crosses, and unmarked mounds.

"What's that?" I'd asked Mother.

She appeared startled. "Oh—nothing. Just a little park, darling."

I knew she was keeping secrets. Dark secrets. Something scary about that piece of land gave me feelings that goose-bumped up my spine the same as when Mother's hand covered my eyes in a picture show: "Don't look now, dear. I'll tell you when . . ."

No image on the screen could be as terrible as what went on in the dark behind Mother's hand. The unknown.

It was Antoine, my playmate in Tuscarora, who revealed the startling information about the "little park."

"You shouldn't ever walk on those graves," he said. "People are planted there."

People? Planted? I concealed my ignorance by remaining silent. But my thoughts were caught in a whirlwind. I knew better than walk in a garden where seeds were planted because then—they wouldn't come up. But—people! The idea was too gruesome to pursue; besides I'd been well-trained in tactics of escape. I avoided that cemetery with the same sense of care as I watched for holes in the street where a child might vanish into an old mining shaft. Pitfalls. Threats. The unknown. The forbidden.

I was beginning to find my aunt's old house forbidding—and boring, too. After leaving the Dunnings, I'd had no playmates. Aunt Williford couldn't stand cats in the house, so poor Snowball had become an outside cat. The Dunnings with my cousin,

Helen, were away on vacation. Aunt Williford tried to keep me entertained while I longed for time alone to invite a Pretend Story.

Gloom rested on the heavy furniture in Aunt Williford's house. Constantly Mother reminded me that we were guests. Children did not put feet on furniture or toss pillows on the floor. The taffeta pillows with small ruffles or hand embroidery formed an orderly row along the back of a faded rose sofa, looking like stern guards in a museum—*do not touch*. Above the sofa hung the painting I thought of as "the tired old man."

"It's a print of a famous painting," my aunt told me, "called *The End of the Trail*."

Framed in a heavy oak wood with a pencil line of gold, the picture disturbed me.

"Why do the man and the horse hang their heads like that?"

"There's no hope left for them," my aunt replied. "It's the end of the trail."

"Why don't they make a new trail through the sage brush?" I remembered such trails in Nevada.

Aunt's Williford's thin lips formed a sad smile. "Sometimes people are too tired to make new trails."

She straightened her sparse figure and attempted to divert my attention by putting a record on the gramophone.

A piece of walnut furniture as tall as I was, the gramophone stood on four short legs with a handle on the side. Sometimes I was allowed to wind it, but Mother always reminded me, "Not too tight, dear."

I've become aware that throughout this narrative I've spoken of my mother as Mother, while at other times I've called her Mom. I believe this has to do with what I was feeling about her at the time. Mother was in charge of me, a kind disciplinarian to be respected. Mom was my pal. So it was Mother who reminded me that I must be careful not to scratch the records and who finally decided I shouldn't play the gramophone at all, because the large round discs were breakable. Each round, black record was enclosed in a paper envelope and through the hole in the center of the paper, I read the titles: "Look for the Silver Lining," "Boy of Mine," "Over There," "Danny Boy," and "There's a Long, Long Trail." I guessed it was the end of the long, long trail that the man and horse had reached.

The sad words of "Danny Boy" coming from the gramophone added to my depression; I sighed and had returned to listlessly winding the gramophone when the door bell rang.

I opened the door to my neighbor Katherine Burke with her mother and her little sister, Rainey. I stared at Katherine thinking she was the prettiest girl I'd ever seen. Her hair, the color of vanilla ice cream, was cut in the latest Irene Castle bob. Katherine had the delicacy of a porcelain doll. She was near my age. Her eyes were so alive, so interested in everything that I never noticed the color until my aunt spoke of them as "a remarkable blue, just like her mother's."

In time I did observe that Katherine and her mother looked alike. Mrs. Burke wore her hair in a bouquet of curls pinned up on top of her head. She had a long neck, usually covered by lace ruffles on her high-collared blouses, climbing up to her dimpled chin. Whispering skirts barely hid her ankles. Sometimes she carried a parasol, but usually she held an artist's easel and paints.

The little sister, Rainey, resembled no one in the family. A dark-skinned child with thin, stringy hair of a mousey shade, she seemed to be forever whining, weeping, or wetting her pants, earning her nickname, Rainey.

That afternoon Mrs. Burke was enrolling Katherine in the ballet school where Helen and I had studied for a brief time: the Johnson School of Classical and Skirt Dancing for Young Misses. She wanted to know if I could go along. Aunt Williford agreed to pay for my lessons. At times I'd heard Mom say to her sister, "If only Shirley could meet some little girls from nice families." I think now this wish motivated my aunt to pay for lessons. I remember her last words before I left the house, "Be sure you learn something. I don't like to waste money."

Dancing of all kinds was the craze that year, although good ballet schools were scarce. I learned something called "fancy dancing," with many Victorian bows and curtsies. Katherine and I watched the ballroom classes where feet flew to faster and faster music. Together we giggled as couples performed strange antics to dances with such names as the Bunny Hop, the Kangaroo, Turkey Trot, and Chicken Scratch.

Soon Katherine and I became best friends. "Chums," my aunt said with an indulgent smile. For the first time I had found a companion whose imagination matched my own. Often she would burst into my story, enhancing the plot with ideas of her own. Most of my stories, at that time, were changing to include death scenes.

In the story of the lost child, Sarah found her way home only to discover her sister was dying.

This story developed in Katherine's large closet where we played our favorite game, funerals. The closet became a chapel with dolls lined up in rows to watch as a shoe box with a "dead doll" was lifted high and carried up the aisle. From Mrs. Burke's classical record collection Katherine chose a Verdi or Bach requiem. Snowball curled up in content beside me.

The house, with soft organ music usually heard in the background, held the forbidding silence and scent of most funeral homes. We whispered. We wept in grief for each "poor soul" carried to the altar. We spoke of "the loved one." From the garden we gathered flowers and took turns serving as soloist or clergyman. When my turn came I sang "Danny Boy"—likely off key. We found it a wonderfully sad game.

Sometimes, during a real funeral, we slipped downstairs into the back of the chapel. Usually a heavy, overly-sweet fragrance of gardenias burdened the room with strange enchantment. Organ tones rumbling from the rear created a mysterious unreality. The bodies borne into that chapel might have all been dolls as far as I was concerned. I believe Katherine felt the same. We knew without really *knowing*. Death had become an inviting fantasy: the flowers grieving, music weeping, while voices intoned a majestic, poetic rhythm; "Ashes to ashes . . ."

People dressed in black. Ladies wearing large veiled hats filed down the aisle. Every face looked solemn and many people cried during the funeral. But afterwards when they met outside, everyone talked and laughed, suggesting that they, too, enjoyed the funeral games.

Mother expressed concern over the time I spent "at the Burke's" and asked many questions. I gathered that Katherine Burke was not one of "the little girls from nice families" that she hoped I would meet. Mother may have been dubious about the funeral home as a proper background. "What do you girls do over there?"

"Oh, we just play with dolls in Katherine's room." That wasn't a lie. I feared if Mother learned we played funeral games she might forbid me going to Katherine's. Grown-ups had strange ideas about so many things.

"Why can't you play over here some of the time?"

I thought about it. "It's more fun over there. I can have Snowball with me and Katherine has more dolls and she can play the gramophone."

"Is her mother usually at home?"

I nodded, and to be honest, added, "Or her father."

Katherine's mother was gone a great deal of the time. Sometimes when at home, she served us tea in her sitting room, filling dainty, china cups and passing small cakes. Often she went off with her paints and the whining Rainey.

Katherine's father, a short, serious man, wore gold-rimmed glasses and spoke in a dry voice. He appeared to adore Katherine and was the only one in either family who knew about the funeral games. Sometimes he would come to Katherine's room while we played and pat her head or joke with us. Often he asked if we were having an open or closed coffin for the day's funeral.

I truly loved Katherine and felt she returned my affection. We were kindred spirits, enjoyed the same love of books, animals, dancing classes, and, best of all, we shared those enchanting rooms of make-believe.

"She is very, very sad . . ." I remember Katherine holding up a dark-haired doll with a chipped nose.

"She must wear her black dress, a hat with a veil, and gloves because today is the funeral," I said.

"Her sister died and her mother died and—and—"

"And her cat died," I supplied.

That scene, and Katherine's words, were to remain in my memory forever.

On the stairs I trembled. What could be so awful that Mother couldn't tell me? Then came the thought—my dad? Fear closed around me like a casket.

Slowly I went down into my aunt's somber parlor. My mother and aunt sat on the rose sofa beneath *The End of the Trail.*

There was a sudden flurry of folding up newspapers. "It's in all the papers," Aunt Williford had said. Again I thought of my father and drew in a long breath.

"Hurry darling," Mother called in a falsely cheerful voice. "I'm taking a holiday. We're going to the city and we'll have ice cream and maybe we'll even go to a picture show! Would you like that?"

I glanced at the stricken face of my aunt and found I needed to breathe through my mouth. I wanted to ask who had died. But never could I break the rules of the game Mother and I played. I must pretend not to know what she didn't want me to know.

I watched her tuck the folded newspaper under one of cushions on the sofa and waited my chance. After breakfast, which I didn't eat, Mother went upstairs to change her clothes and my aunt went out in the garden. With shaky hands I unfolded the newspapers. I didn't have to look beyond the first page. The story leaped out in headlines:

MURDER IN BERKELEY FUNERAL HOME

The story told that a Mr. Robert Burke, who owned the funeral home, confessed to shooting his wife and youngest daughter. His lawyers pleaded temporary insanity. He was being held in prison.

Pictures of Katherine's pretty mother with the two children stared back at me. "Taken a year ago," the caption read, "when Louise Burke's paintings were shown at a local gallery."

Tears dropped on the newspaper. I could no longer see the print. I could see Katherine. She was holding up the doll with the chipped nose and she said, "She is very sad. Her mother died . . . and her sister died . . ."

The papers fell to the floor and I ran sobbing to the front door.

My aunt caught me in the entry. "Where—?" she started.

"Let me go! Let me go," I screamed. "I have to see Katherine."

She held me, making crooning noises until Mother came and took me in her arms.

"Darling, Katherine's not there. Her grandmother came last night and took her to Orinda."

"Where's Orinda? Can't I visit Katherine? Please. Oh please."

Somewhere Katherine was alone and terrified. She needed me.

I was told I must wait for no one knew where Katherine was. My aunt promised to find out.

Later I was to wonder why I hadn't written a note to Katherine and put it in the Burke's mail box. But I suppose I was too young to think of this. No one made such a suggestion.

I continued to grieve over Katherine's loss and my loss of her friendship. I understood now why Mother tried to keep me from knowing that lives can end suddenly and in a horrible way.

By eavesdropping on my mother and aunt, I learned that Mr. Burke was "wildly jealous" of his pretty wife.

"And perhaps," my aunt said in her sharpest tones, "she wasn't as perfect as she appeared with her parasol and frills. Artists don't have the same morals as other folks."

"There are rumors," Mother said, "that Rainey wasn't his child."

Did she mean Rainey was adopted? Not really Katherine's sister?

Katherine. I kept asking when I could see her. Mother continued to put me off and finally, she told me that Katherine had moved away and was not coming back.

"We're going to move, too," she said. "We're taking a flat with Kitty and Helen down by Lake Merritt. You'll have your cousin to play with once more. Won't that be nice?"

I knew then that I would never see Katherine again—because Mother didn't want me to. For a long time, my imaginary world became a place obsessed with grief and death.

"It's all so morbid," Mother told my aunt. "I must get her away soon, so she'll forget."

But I didn't forget.

Oakland's Upper Crumbs

It was because of Cleveland School that Mother gloried over finding the flat on First Avenue.

She raved to Aunt Kitty about it being the best school district in Oakland. Aunt Kitty agreed that the flat was reasonable and that they should take it before it was gone.

My first question when I learned we were to share a house with Aunt Kitty and Helen was, "Which of us will be the guests?"

I was relieved to hear Mother say, "Neither of us."

"Won't Uncle Will come, too?"

Mother told me that the Dunnings had separated and added, "For a time, at least."

"But why?" I had a myriad of whys. The Dunnings! But I'd never heard them quarrel, never heard a cross word spoken between them.

As usual I was told I was too young to understand. I realized my curiosity could be satisfied only through eavesdropping.

I had the chance one Sunday afternoon when the aunts collected in Ann Williford's parlor beneath that picture of the old man at the end of his trail. Helen and I crouched on the stair, an ideal place for listening, unobserved.

Five of Mother's seven sisters were present. Aunt Bessie, the youngest, still lived with my grandparents and attended school in Hanford, California. Aunt Elli, the oldest, lived with her husband on a ranch in Lodi, California. But Aunt Agnes and Uncle Warren had sold the peach ranch and moved to Oakland. Warren, on the advice of his brother-in-law Alfred Williford, bought a laundry truck and went into business for himself. At that time, there were several companies eager to take laundry jobs from independent drivers.

I couldn't see my relatives' faces from the stair, but I recognized Agnes's confident voice, rounded with merriment. I never heard her mention the loss of the ranch. Now she said something like, "Will always had an eye for a pretty women, Kitty. You know that. And he married one when he found you in the ice cream parlor." She tried to reassure her sister that Will would come back and something she said stayed with me. "He'll return meek as an old cow looking for his stall."

Between sobs, Aunt Kitty said she knew Will had met a pretty dental nurse. Beside me, Helen sniffed back tears. I put a warning finger to my lips.

I can still hear Aunt Williford snap, "If he tries to come back, I hope you'll have spunk enough to turn him out."

This only served to bring a fresh storm of sobs from Aunt Kitty.

I glanced at Helen, who sullenly assured me that her dad would return soon. I'd began to doubt that my dad would ever return from the mines.

So we moved to First Avenue and became a household of four females and one white cat, Snowball. The rent was split. Mother continued to nurse as the influenza epidemic worsened by the fall of 1918. The Oakland Auditorium had been turned into a hospital for the emergency.

Without Will Dunning, the happy times I remembered with his family were gone. Helen became increasingly peevish, and we quarreled a great deal. It seemed that Kitty always took sides with Helen now.

I shed lots of tears on First Avenue. I have memories of sitting out on the front steps of the flat, holding Snowball and watching the darkening street at twilight for Mother.

When I saw her round the corner, walking briskly, I raced to meet her and to feel her love rescue me again and again from despair. I believed there was little in the whole world impossible for my mother. She could take care of everything. Separated from her, I was in jeopardy.

This sense of insecurity grew when I started going to Cleveland School. To get to school from our flat, I needed to walk along Lake Merritt's east shore for a quarter of a mile, then turn up the hill to pass an endless white fence that bordered the Borax Smith estate—the fellow known as 20-mule–team Borax, whose team appeared on Mom's box of washing powder. My legs ached before I came to the neatly clipped hedges of old mansions set far back from the street. Dreading that school as I did, I can still follow my dragging footsteps all the way to the school yard.

The girls in my class formed a clique. These girls arrived at the school gate every morning driven by a parent in an elegant motor car, sometimes even by chauffeurs. I supposed you had to be awfully rich to own a motor car.

At that time Oakland's social set occupied the shores of Lake Merritt and extended northeast into the district of Piedmont. While First Avenue was only one block from the lake, in social strata it was star-distance between Piedmont and the business section of First Avenue—the gap between "them" and "us." At a wider gap, the "colored," as we referred to African-Americans, occupied run-down homes in West Oakland. These once-elegant Victorians had been built by Oakland's founders. No colored children attended Cleveland School.

❧

At that school I was sent into Miss Heiner's third grade class.

"Humph," Miss Heiner snorted after looking at my transcript. She said something about my having no more than a few weeks of schooling and added in a tone of accusation, "and you're eight years old."

"I'll be nine in five and a half months," I offered, to set the records straight. Apparently she looked upon my youth with scorn.

Miss Heiner had been a high school teacher and she talked to the third grade class as though they were ninth graders.

She said she had no idea where I might belong but she'd test me for third grade. She had a mannerism of twisting her mouth into a sneer and talked out of the left side. "My third-grade students have been together since kindergarten." She warned me that they were advanced and that she had no time for extra instruction.

Miss Heiner was homely in the most distinctive way, for while scores of pretty faces I've known through the decades are forgotten, her image remains unfaded in memory's pocket.

She steps out of that image for me now. A note of complaint creeps in and out of her rasping voice, a reminder of failure to meet expectations. She paces the room, an angular figure in a plain, dark skirt and white blouse. If upset over current events, she claws the air with her skeeter-bug fingers while she lectures.

That first day she quizzed me on arithmetic. I could always recall those sums pinned up on the outhouse walls. Apparently satisfied with my proficiency, she gave me a passing grade. A week later, she bid me write a story. It was to be a story about my experience at Cleveland School.

I will never forget sitting in that classroom with a pen gripped in my stiffened fingers and that sheet of blank paper on the desk beneath my wrist. My entrance into the third grade—or kindergarten—depended on what I put on that piece of paper! But whatever could I say about my experience at Cleveland School?

I thought about what had happened so far.

My classmates had attended the same school since kindergarten. They met at social functions, attended the same dancing classes, parties, and musicals.

And, naturally, there was a bully. Her name was California, called "Cally" by her group. Except for her, I wouldn't have minded being a loner. Since I'd started school, overly dressed, in Tuscarora, I'd never belonged to a group. In spite of my missed schooling, I kept up with the others that first week, probably because of insatiable reading habits and a love of studying.

Cally was the leader. A short, squarely built girl, she had black bangs that drew an uncompromising line above small, mean eyes.

Once at recess I was swinging from bar to bar on the jungle gym when Cally arrived. I ignored her. She climbed up on the bars above me and suddenly I felt her foot grind down on my fingers. I let go with a cry and banged my head on a bar before landing in the sawdust. This confrontation with injustice left bruises on my spirit. *But I hadn't done anything to her.* I kept asking myself, *Why didn't she like me?*

"You stay off these bars, you hear?" she demanded. "You don't belong here."

For a time I met Helen at recess and we went off by ourselves. But Helen was sickly and Kitty worried over the influenza epidemic, so Helen's attendance became sporadic.

Usually I wandered around the schoolyard alone, trying to appear as if I had a destination. But I was driven indoors by the rains that had started in September to overrun gutters and flood the streets. In the library, I could escape in a book.

Now as I thought back over what had happened to me that first week at school, I decided I'd make up a happy story for Miss Heiner. I'd write about a girl whose family had lots of money so no one could say she didn't belong at this school.

I wrote, "Sally Had Many Friends at School."

And there I stopped. I was aware of sounds around me: the click of the clock when the hands moved, rustling of papers, whispering. I was further distracted by movement: someone got up to sharpen a pencil. Miss Heiner paced down the aisles.

I tried to imagine myself back at The Sandy Shore where new stories flowed along with the river. But something had happened to my imagination during this unhappy week. Actually it had been a long time since my fingers clutched The Wad with the rising excitement of a story needing utterance.

The more I tried to bring up a story here in this crowded classroom, the more impossible it became. Words for me had become lifeless stones.

I recalled my Dad teaching me to memorize before I learned to read. He taught me to recite long passages from *Evangeline*, from *The Tempest, Midsummer Night's Dream,* the *Rubaiyat*, and many other poems.

Once Mother told him he should be teaching me to read instead of wasting time on things I'd never use.

I remember Dad's argument, for of course, they argued. "Once the Turk learns to read," he said "words will shift from play things to hard work."

He felt it necessary for me to have "a comprehensible collection of words to play with before bubbles turned into stones."

Now I guessed that was what had happened. With every jumping click of the clock, I stiffened as if I, too, were turning to stone sitting behind that small desk.

Finally the bell rang. The paper remained blank except for one short sentence and a spot where a tear had fallen. I looked up at Miss Heiner standing over me and wondered if I'd be put back into kindergarten.

She snorted, wrinkling her nose. Then she commented that I hadn't made much progress. However she gave me a week to write my story at home.

She returned to her desk, picked up a newspaper and faced the class. "It's happened! Just as I predicted. Right here in America!" She held the front page of the *San Francisco Chronicle* up for the class to see.

Headlines read: "U.S. troops rushed to Seattle. Soviets blamed."

"This is a city struck between the eyes," she read from the editorial. "It was dazed by a complete business paralysis of the general strike. 'This is Bolshevism,' say its citizens."

Talk of Bolsheviks had began to dominate the news while peace talks with our European allies were underway. Editorials warned that the Bolsheviks threatened to take over every country in the world. As a result a plethora of American flags fluttered from schools, clubs, and homes. Special patriotic entertainment claimed the land like wild mustard.

But I was more concerned about my own enemies.

One day at recess Cally and her gang circled me and I knew I was in trouble.

"My mother told me you don't have a father."

"I do, too." I remembered what Mother had told me to say. "My father is working on his gold mine and will be visiting us soon."

"Gold mine!" Cally exclaimed and her friends shared glances.

"If your father owns a gold mine you must be rich," she said, looking at me with new respect.

I wasn't one to let an opportunity slip by. "Oh," I said with a shrug of one shoulder, "Dad owns several gold mines in Nevada."

"You must be awful rich, huh?"

I dismissed this question with another shrug.

My status at school changed that day. I was invited to join in games with jacks or jump rope. Cally stood back with respect while I climbed the monkey bars. Still I knew I had no friends. Although I felt badly over this, I was far more concerned over the composition that, as the deadline approached, my fingers refused to write. Did this mean my storytelling ability was gone?

What would Miss Heiner do if I failed to bring her the composition? I regarded her with a mixture of bewilderment, respect, and terror. School, I'd decided, like the dentist, was a punishment children must bear. But of all schools, Cleveland must be the worst.

Rain continued and the flu epidemic took its toll both in army camps and in the cities. The major news debated the German peace offensive and the League of Nations. Miss Heiner explained that Germany was prepared to talk peace with us in the west because we were winning there, but that the United States should not think of talking peace until we were equally successful in the east, especially in Russia.

With the war nearing an end, peace talks received mixed reviews. But Miss Heiner's views never varied. On a Wednesday, in her usual whine, she asked how many were going to the Flying Circus air show.

When I told Mother that our teacher wanted us to see the Flying Circus, she agreed that we could go. Aunt Kitty and Mother would take Helen and me.

"It will be educational," Mom said.

That night while I sat at the dining room table, struggling once more to get that despised composition onto paper, Mother asked if I knew a girl at school named California.

I must have asked why.

Mom said she'd been getting notes and invitations from this girl's mother. "She must think we're rich."

I told my mother and aunt about the gold mines and they laughed until they wiped tears. Then I learned that invitations to charity balls and requests for donations for the starving Armenians flooded our mail box.

From then on, Aunt Kitty teased Mom on many occasions. "You can afford to pay, Tess. You own those gold mines."

Being a gold miner's child made school life easier for me, if not happier.

All that week rain overran gutters and flooded the streets. Mom and Aunt Kitty expressed hope that it wouldn't rain on the air show.

The Flying Circus was to appear over the Presidio on Sunday. The rain never let up for the British aviators, but in the British tradition, they "carried on." We stood with the crowd on the slushy grass, umbrellas folded, hands shielding our eyes from the downpour, while we watched the awesome two-seaters dart out of the dark clouds. A prolonged chorus of "ooohs!" from observers greeted each small plane that swept down so daringly over the field.

Up to this time planes were rare enough to bring people to a halt on the street.

"Look there's an airship!" someone would cry.

Then the flurry of shoppers on Market Street would halt as suddenly as the end of a newsreel. It was a common sight to see people standing, heads tilted upward, arms serving as a visor. The wonder of it—human beings away up there in the air, flying like birds!

To fly like a bird has been part of my fantasies since the first stories came to me on The Divide's sandy shore. I found the air show the most exciting scene I had ever witnessed.

But on that rainy Sunday, while enjoying shivers of excitement, I hugged fear close to me. Sometimes I hid my eyes while planes circled around one another so close they seemed bound to collide. I swallowed hard when, with a sudden roar of motors, those planes swooped down close to our heads.

Even more chilling than the roar of motors was the ra-ta-ta-tat of gun fire as the planes demonstrated battle maneuvers.

"Where are they shooting from?" I screamed at Mother over the racket.

She didn't know. Following the show, General Charles Frederick Lee explained the new Fokker machine gun to the audience.

Later Mother interpreted. The newly perfected gun had some kind of gear that allowed the men to shoot bullets between the spinning propellers of the plane. That sounded impossible to both Mother and me. Why, the propellers spun so fast you couldn't see the blades!

It had become a race, Mother explained, not only in flying machines but also in gunnery, as to who could direct the most effective fire on the enemy.

"Wouldn't you love to fly?" Helen asked, on the ferry boat taking us back across the bay where the big, gray warships pointed cannons toward our boat.

I hesitated. "Yes, like the sea gulls, without any guns."

I looked up at some gulls flying above the deck and then I thought about those guns filling the birds' air space with shells. Why that was horrible! Helen said something and I didn't hear her. I leaned on the boat's railing and gazed up at the clouds. A great band of sea gulls gathered there, all screaming at once. They were meeting to discuss the danger of the aviators shooting in bird territory. Their children weren't safe any longer in air space. One bird, they decided, had to be a hero and fly in front of a darting plane. If the pilot could be blinded for a second, he might crash and that would stop future air shows and killings. I, a great gray bird, was elected to fly in front of a darting plane to blind a pilot in the Air Show.

When I returned home that night, the old excitement sent me dashing to the table where I wrote my sea gull story. I knew then that I could still tell stories but I had to feel excited about something. I doubted if Miss Heiner would accept this story because it wasn't about my experience at Cleveland School. The next morning I was joyfully surprised to receive a gold star on my paper, where my teacher had written one word, "imaginative"!

The rest of that week, small boys "flew" around the school yard, arms extended for wings, making motor noises and ra-ta-ta-tatting one another with machine gun fire. The brigadier's show must have made more of an impression than any of the lessons learned that semester.

One of these young aviators charged up behind me in the corridor, firing his machine gun and shouted, "Charlie's dead." I thought he'd said "Shirley's dead."

Then I remembered that the expression meant my petticoat showed. I ducked into the girls' room and in the privacy of a cubicle discovered a broken strap. Aunt Williford had made the petticoat out of the finest lawn, trimmed with lace, but it had undergone many a washing since my birthday last March. I had no safety pin. What was I to do? At any moment the bell would ring. Forced to decision, I removed my faded, plaid skirt and white blouse, wiggled out of the tight petticoat, rolled it up as small as possible and tucked it behind the toilet.

Guilt pursued me down the corridor where I was two minutes late for class. Mother worked hard. I couldn't afford to throw away petticoats that only needed mending. Would she be cross?

The day wore on and it was late afternoon during math class, with the gray rain drumming the windows, when one of the girls who worked in the office walked in. Stricken, I saw my dingy petticoat in her hand. Then she unfurled the shameful garment before the class. Miss Heiner, with her usual sneer, demanded, "Does this—belong to anyone here?"

I cringed down in my seat, pretending to study the blackboard. A few girls behind me giggled and no wonder. This rag was certain evidence that penury lurked in their midst. My status as a gold miner's child wobbled in the balance.

Still the office girl held the petticoat, and waited. "This" she said in a tone of contempt, "was found in the girls' room."

"Why don't you leave it with me for the time being?" Miss Heiner whined.

When she took it the awful thought hit me, *Aunt Williford always embroidered initials on her gifts.* Dread, hot as a fever, burned into my skin. Miss Heiner would look down and read *S.P.* I closed my eyes and wished that the school would burn down before she could say, "Shirley Pedlar, this must be yours."

I snuck a glance at Miss Heiner. Sure enough she was examining the petticoat. Then, she looked directly at me. *She knew*! I felt the hot blood rush to my face. For a second the sharp eyes held mine. Quickly I looked down, twisting my fingers together in my lap and prayed for an earthquake, a hurricane, anything. My teacher said nothing, and when I looked again the wretched garment was out of sight. My heart warmed toward Miss Heiner.

(Years later this incident would appear in a short story.)

All that day I worried that Mom would send me to ask Miss Heiner for the petticoat. That evening I ran through the rain in tears to meet her. Probably I blurted out, "Something awful happened today . . ."

When I had finished relating the story, Mother surprised me by breaking into laughter. It must have been incongruous, after a day of nursing the sick and dying, to hear her solemn child give such tragic proportions to a petticoat tale.

Relieved I joined in Mom's merriment, for "Mother" had become "Mom" again that night. By the time we reached the front porch we were hugging each other between fits of uncontrolled laughter.

Later I was to realize that material belongings were of short-term importance to Mother. As hard as she worked for "nice things," once she acquired some coveted possession, a candlewick bedspread or a fine china vase, the value appeared to diminish. I know she was sincere in wanting to surround me with beautiful things and to give me a life removed from the drudgery she had known. For herself, it often seemed that it was important only to be in a position to have something to discard, to briefly enjoy the right of the rich to profligacy.

I can hear her saying merrily, "Let's just pitch the old thing." And she would roll up a faded dress or some disliked garment and toss it across the room with an air of wicked abandon.

But about this time, our personal lives were upset once more and anything that happened on the planet beyond First Avenue lost importance. Uncle Will, as Aunt Agnes had predicted, drove up to the flat one day with a huge bouquet of roses for Aunt Kitty. He had purchased a new home for her and Helen in the recently developed suburb of Fruitvale. Soon Aunt Kitty was singing a little tuneless song as she polished Will's shoes.

Aunt Kitty said that Mother and I must stay with them until we found a place we could afford.

But Mother refused. She was determined not to change schools for me and told Kitty that we'd find rooms somewhere. Then she said something that made my heart dance on tiptoe. She was going to write to Dad and tell him he'd have to send us money or come home and support his family.

Would he come?

Thanksgiving was approaching when Mother and I moved into a rooming house overlooking Lake Merritt. The landlady had to be talked into taking children. She was adamant about not taking cats, so poor Snowball went to visit the Dunnings. I was crying about this when Dad's letter arrived.

I couldn't believe he was coming home!

Truce
November 11, 1918

I HAD RECEIVED only two short letters from Dad during the eight months since Mother and I had come to California. Once Aunt Kitty said, "Elmer Pedlar is a fine man, but he's no family man." That I guessed was true. Often I wondered if he missed me as much as I missed him. Of course he had the life at The Divide to comfort him, while I had only Cleveland School and loneliness.

Dad had no trouble finding a job in the shipyards, such jobs being plentiful in California during those war years. But I didn't expect him to stay long.

It is likely my parents were attempting a reconciliation. While we had a peaceful interlude we became a family of three. How I dreaded the time when they would start quarreling; then I would be left out as my parents became gripped in a contest that involved only the two of them. How I feared the sound of harsh voices bringing on the old threat—with its chilling certainty—that one day Dad would leave and never return.

And it wasn't long before I heard that harsh note in their voices. Dad subscribed to the old idea that one paid cash for purchases rather than run up bills. He was a fanatic on that subject. Mother, having been denied the pleasures of shopping for a long time, reveled in credit.

She had purchased new outfits for me to start Cleveland School. For once my clothes did not differ from the others. And she bought a new outfit for herself to wear when she attended the parents' meetings.

On the first of that month the arguments started. "How are we going to pay these bills?" Dad's voice raised in anger. "Holy Moses, three dollars for a child's shoes! Have you gone out of your mind, Tess?"

Whenever he called her "Tess," instead of "Tereda," it meant he was really upset with her.

And Mother would snap back. "Do you want your child to go to school barefoot? Don't forget I'm working, too. The bills will get paid. They always do."

After Dad returned to California, I found a sad change in him, but far more sad was the distance wedged in between us by our long separation. He looked older, and I remembered he was more than twenty years Mom's senior. Never before had I noticed gray in the black curly hair receding from his high forehead, or the deepening parenthesis around his sensitive mouth. But what could have happened to make us strangers? I was no longer the accepting child who held his crippled hand and slipped through the brush to see the beaver. I suppose he recognized a daughter who looked at him with new awareness. Surely he felt guilt over his long absence and, perhaps, imagined criticism in my glance.

It was not criticism I felt, only bewilderment and pain. I was no longer his "Little Turk." He called me "honey" now. My legs were too long. I felt shy, awkward, and worst of all, so far removed from him. Besides, I bore my share of guilt: I had become Mother's child. I doubted if Dad and I could ever feel the same bond again, and nothing saddened me more.

November 11, 1918, was a day I remember vividly, for it was one of the rare times I spent alone with him. As the influenza epidemic mounted, Mom worked long hours nursing at the Oakland Auditorium. Usually Mrs. Riggs, the landlady, stayed with me. Of course it was far nicer having my dad, who was working the swing shift at Moore's Shipyards.

For breakfast that morning Dad cooked scrambled eggs with raisin toast. I was still in my nightgown and robe. I could see he struggled to find something to talk about. I tried, too.

Was it the city, I wondered, that made him a stranger? I imagined my real dad and a real "me" back in the sage-smelling woods. We held hands, swinging arms on one of our walks. Words flowed as naturally as the mountain water racing down the stream alongside of us on its way to the sea.

That morning I suppose we tried to talk about the animals: Minniehaha; the chipmunks; Nemo and Frisky; Red, the robin; and a jackrabbit that Dad called Pitcher, because little pitchers have big ears. And he spoke of Smokey.

"We'll get another cat," he said.

"The landlady won't allow pets." I told him about Snowball, who had to be a guest with the Dunnings.

He gave me a quick look, anger in his face. Then he said we'd have a place of our own soon and people would not be telling us what we could do.

I nodded, not believing him. Mom had been telling me that for too many years.

I asked him if that meant he was not going back to Nevada.

"Would you like me to stay?" Were his faded blue eyes watery or did I imagine it?

"Oh yes, yes!"

Did he mean it? I was afraid to hope. Then I remembered how he hated the city. He must be feeling as sad as I had after leaving our mountain home.

He washed the dishes and, in silence, I wiped them. We went into the small parlor facing Lake Merrit. Dad sat in a arm chair with a rip in the leather where the stuffing poked out. It looked like a snowshoe rabbit thrusting his head out of a hole beneath the arm rest. I sprawled on the rug.

He handed me the *Saturday Evening Post*. With a ghost of his old grin, he reminded me how I always tried to beat him to the

Post in the cabin. "There's an amusing P. G. Wodehouse story in this issue."

I nodded and reached for that time again with my smile to him. Had he been trying to rediscover me, too? Why did it feel so impossible?

We were sitting there reading, likely both wishing that we could slide time backwards and find the same old Dad and Turk. That was when voices began to shout below the windows. "Ex-tra! Ex-tra! Read all about it. War . . ."

Quickly Dad rose and went over to pull back the lace curtains. I couldn't understand what the newsboys were shouting, but I heard excitement in their voices.

Dad's light blue eyes reflected that excitement when he turned to me. "Honey, the war is over!" He told me the Armistice had finally been signed. I was to don my "best bib and tucker." This called for a celebration and he suggested we go out and buy all the popcorn the vendor had. "We'll make this a day you'll remember."

My heart jumped rope while I scrambled into my wool jumper and sweater. What a thrilling thing to do! Unexpected things were such fun.

Dad reminded me to wear my flu mask. We wore them to school until the schools were closed the previous month because of the epidemic. Dad didn't bother with his mask, although people were warned daily to wear masks to help stop the epidemic. I guessed he would try to keep the freedom he cherished for as long as possible.

When we left the rooming house, there was a mob gathering across the street at Lakeside Park. People ran down the stairs from apartments and houses facing the lake. Despite the cold, the air smelled like Fourth of July. But with all the horns, whistles, and shouting going on, it sounded like New Year's Eve.

I held tightly to Dad's rough hand, enjoying the familiar touch of his finger stumps.

We fell in step with the crowd. People looked strange. Bundled in mufflers, scarves and caps, nearly everyone we passed wore white gauze masks. But that didn't matter so much because in Oakland you couldn't recognize people anyway. There were too many of them. In Tuscarora on the Fourth of July or most any-time, we would see friends and call, "Hello, Miss Plumb," or "Hello, Pie," and greet old Mrs. Rose or our friends, the Primeauxs. I missed Antoine and wondered how he was celebrating tonight. Then I thought of my mother and wondered if she knew the war was over. I guessed there was no time to celebrate in a hospital.

On the lake sparklers sprayed ovals of tiny, glittering stars from small boats. Firecrackers, smelling of gun powder, arced from the shore to explode over the water.

Hawkers with trays of souvenirs shoved past us, shouting, "Serpentine, confetti, horns.

Newsboys shouted, "Ex-tra! Armistice signed! Read all about it."

Dad stopped to buy a paper with bold black headlines: THE WAR IS OVER!

"You'll want to hang on to this paper," he told me. "Someday you'll show it to your grandchildren."

Strangers hugged each other. A man lifted me up in the air, gave me a balloon, and dashed off. That mood of exuberance crackled and spread like a fire in dry sagebrush. Only the chimes from the Congregational Church sounded solemn notes.

Many men in uniform mixed with the now jostling crowd. I remembered a boy at school whose father had been killed. There were other reminders that this was not a happy time for every-one—such as the soldier across the street on crutches with an empty pant leg.

A girl about my age held the soldier's hand. Had her father been away a long time? Was there, between them, that painful gap where something familiar was missing?

We stopped before the two-wheeled popcorn wagon, looking like an oversized wheelbarrow, and watched Jolly Corn jumping above the built-in stove. I wished I might warm my hands over that stove. The man filled big paper cones and poured fragrant melted butter over them.

From the bandstand in Lakeside Park, a medley of "Yankee Doodle," "Hinky Dinky Parlez Vous," and "Over There" burst out on the morning air. The crowd joined in singing or blowing horns and whistles. Forgotten flu masks became necklaces. But I kept mine on because Mother had said I must wear it on the street. I wished I could blow horns and shout with the others but I would never dare to break Mother's rules.

Voices and noisemakers grew louder and louder as the crowd swelled to fill streets and sidewalks. Dad jerked his necktie loose and unfastened the top button on his shirt.

I wondered if he'd seem more like Dad if he wore the old patched pants with a necktie for a belt and a faded shirt—clothes that let him whistle and sing.

Once I stepped off the sidewalk and found the grass soggy beneath my shoes. Yellow leaves floated down from the elms. Near the tree trunk, among the leaves, a dead robin thrust up spindly claws in protest.

Here grass, green from a wet fall, water, birds, and many of the trees were the same as the high desert, yet here that combination could never be more than a city park. Surely I was too young to realize that some things cannot be transplanted without sorrow, without loss: plants that die in a foreign clime, animals of the wild who fail to survive a zoo. Yet I recall the scene and my sadness.

I nestled my icy hand into Dad's. He bought a red striped horn for me and asked why I didn't blow it.

"Mother told me to keep my mask on," I told him, and hoped I hadn't hurt his feelings.

He frowned slightly, perhaps because I wasn't his child anymore, then he nodded.

Finally he took the heavy gold watch on the chain from his vest pocket. "Well Hon, had enough? Think it's about time we head for our warm nest."

I agreed. We turned back. We seemed to be going against the tide of merrymakers. Dad put an arm around me to hold me close to his side as people bumped against us, laughing, shouting, and crying. They nearly knocked me down. Fear heightened my excitement. Had everyone gone crazy? On and on the crowd came like stampeding animals. Louder and louder the shouts grew to rise above the screech of horns, shrill whistles, pop of balloons and firecrackers. A cold breeze carrying the smell of the crowd and of danger touched my neck, lifted my hair, and sent a chill down from between my shoulders. Would I be crushed, smothered? Would Mother approve of my being out on this dangerous street? During Dad's absence I'd lost a streak of reckless adventure.

Through all the racket a sudden yowl snatched my attention. Then I saw the terrified kitten. It cringed in the street between the feet of the crowd. Someone must have stepped on it.

"Daddy!"

He saw it, too. Gripping me close to him he pushed through the crowd and swooped up the forlorn cat, tucking it under his coat. The cat continued to "meow."

"Is it hurt?" I must have cried.

Dad replied that he thought it was only somewhat "disembobulated" and in need of nourishment.

Disembobulated was a Dad-word, one I associated with *Alice in Wonderland,* and so I felt reassured.

When, at last, we closed the door of our rooms, Dad put the small kitten down on the rug.

It was a rainbow cat with a gray body, white paws, and head, legs, and tail of marbled orange over brown. Its ribs were showing. The tail was three times the length of its small body.

I was afraid it was starving.

Dad assured me that could be remedied. Then he said something like, "He's a good cat. His colors show a fine tolerance for felines of all colors and classes."

My father's manner of speaking does not translate well into today's idiom. In that time before radio, many people took pride in an individual way of expression. The most eloquent speakers found their way into politics. Dad took pleasure in words and in arranging them to convey some thought, often humorous. Although I guessed at meanings, his unusual phrasing and choice of words delighted me. After all these years he continues to speak to me through some distant acoustical cloud.

I helped him open a can of salmon, an appropriate meal for cats at ten cents a can. We talked the entire time. The cat waited with continual demands that we hurry.

When I asked Dad what we should name the cat, he suggested Truce. "Since we found him on Armistice Day."

"The landlady won't let us keep Truce," I mourned.

Dad snorted. He said no landlady would dictate to us on such matters. Truce was a member of our family now.

"B-but we're only guests," I explained. I guessed Dad hadn't been in the city long enough to know you couldn't do as you liked here. So I told him about being guests all the time and how hard it was not to have animals or to be free to swing from trees or turn cartwheels.

Dad's expression turned grim. "Don't worry, Little Turk." He promised me that we would find a house. "It may not be much, but we'll be able to kick up our heels and have our pets."

He'd called me "Turk"!

I climbed up on his lap and hugged him. I doubted if he could raise a wand and produce a house any sooner than Mom could. Still I was happy. Truce managed to shift time backward so we were Dad and Turk again.

"Truce acts like he's found a home," Dad said.

The multicultured cat, stomach full, was playfully pulling the white stuffing out of the torn leather of the arm chair.

Mom might be distressed. But Dad and I rocked with laughter as we watched the antics of a cat whose joy, that night, matched our own.

The Little Nest

WE HAD SUCCEEDED for some time in keeping Truce a secret. But one morning the landlady caught Dad going down the back stairs with the sandbox. She demanded we get rid of the cat. Dad refused. She gave us a month's notice to move. Christmas was only a few weeks away.

Except for one Christmas, I remember little about the holidays during those years. I suppose we usually were guests of some of the relatives.

The Christmas I remember, when we went to the Dunnings for dinner, may have been the first time we took the trolley car down Fruitvale Avenue to Helen's new home. Other than the brightly decorated tree, I find I'm remembering more about the house than the holiday.

The white stucco bungalow was built in the newest Spanish style. Mother and I thought it elegant. Best of all, the bathtub had griffin feet with claws. A long driveway led to the rear of the house with a garage so small the Will King stuck halfway out. The modern kitchen followed the fashion for built-in appliances: a breakfast nook, a big ice box, even a built-in ironing board. Of course, the house had a "guest room" for me—the perennial guest. I may have spent the night. I know I was happy to see Snowball.

Around two weeks later, Dad returned to the boarding house on Sunday afternoon and announced that he had a surprise for us. Then he said the unforgettable words: "How would you and Mother like to take a ride to Fruitvale and see your new home?"

New home! I was struck dumb. Could it really be happening? My first thought was we could have both Truce and Snowball. I wondered if the bathtub would have griffin feet. How could Dad afford a house? Then I remembered he'd brought a flask of gold from Nevada. Had gold prices gone up?

Mother appeared as horrified as I was delighted. "You bought a house?" she cried. "Without letting me see it?"

"It's no mansion, Tess," he replied. He called her Tess when afraid of her. He said something about it being a start, a way to gather some equity. "And the Little Turk can have her pets and not be hushed all the time."

I threw my arms around him in a big bear hug.

"All right," Mother sounded resigned. "How much did you pay?"

Dad said she wouldn't believe it. The house cost less than $1500 and Dad's friend, Reeves, had arranged for us to move in with no down payment. Dad said our payments would be less than the rent in the rooming house.

"It must be a chicken shack," Mother replied. "Let's go look at it."

We took the street car that went out East 14th Street. Dad looked worried, Mother furious. My hands became moist. My parents had nothing to say to each other so I asked a lot of questions to make the awful silence go away. Yes, Dad told me I would have my own room. No, the bathtub didn't have griffin feet but that was okay since it wasn't going anyplace.

No giant or evil spirit from my story books—not Caliban, Goliath, or Gog—threatened me as much as the invisible presence of resentment between my parents. In the silence this presence would swell, not like a balloon but like a dirigible, to quickly crowd a room with antagonism.

When we stepped off the street car at Harrington Avenue, the dirigible went with us while we walked down that long line of houses on each side of the street. Mother's expression "chicken shacks" suited these wooden structures well. Narrow shingled houses with neglected yards crowded together. In silence we went, the three of us, past scrubby lawns with tricycles and abandoned dolls scattered out front.

"They're not all sold yet," Dad suggested hopefully, "so you can choose from what's left."

"Thanks," Mother retorted. "Then I'll take the last one. At least we'll have one foot out of poverty row."

By then the dirigible filled the twilight and left no air to breathe. I doubted if the chicken house could hold that much resentment. But it did.

The small houses were built like a train, with one room in front of the other. My bedroom was in front of the house and led into the small living room with a door to the outside. Next came the kitchen with a breakfast nook barely big enough for two people. My parents slept on a screened-in porch behind the kitchen. Fixtures in the bathroom crowded against one another. This room, along with two closets for brooms and a water heater, occupied one side of the kitchen, probably to save plumbing expense.

~

"Elmer, you forgot to close that door again! Am I supposed to enjoy breakfast gazing at a toilet?"

Dad would sigh and get up to close the door. "Don't know why that bothers you so much. Not a bad-looking toilet as toilets go. You might consider sitting on the other side of the table, Tereda?"

~

Dad's job on the swing shift at the shipyards meant he went to work at midnight and arrived home at dawn. Mother insisted on getting up to fix his breakfast.

"What would you like to eat, Elmer?"

"Oh, just toss me a bun, Tereda."

From my single bed in the tiny room at the front of the house, I listened to their whispers and gazed out at the strangest hour: no longer dark, it was not yet light. Stars and moon hung in a colorless heaven while rooftops became almost visible. It should be called "shift swing," I decided. It was like the pause when you're drawn way back in the swing and held in anticipation until the pusher lets go.

In high desert country, such as The Divide, the vast world is held back in the pause of night before it swings, then a soft gray light comes over the purple mountains to silver the sage brush as far as the eye can see.

In the mountains of Bull Run, pine trees display stained glass windows between the branches. Colors change slowly, from neutral to the palest lavender; then light tests all its blues before choosing the shell of the robin's egg.

Dad worked hard but, at least, he began the day at the right place.

"Mom, these houses are bigger than our cabin in the mountains." I would look at Dad. He has done this for me.

"We can do what we like again. Have animals and not have to be guests."

Mom seldom answered. Furious at Dad for not consulting her, she became cross whenever the subject was brought up. She must have been very unhappy to be cross so much of the time during those years.

She quarreled with a supervisor at the hospital over the number of blankets she put on a patient. Angry at being criticized, she quit and went to work in Capwell's Department Store.

Once she said, "It's necessary to work hard if you want to get ahead."

Ahead of whom, I'd wondered.

But by the time I was ten, I knew. She wanted to get ahead of the poor. The pillbox house might look as if we were behind the poor, but I enjoyed the freedom.

I did not start Jefferson School immediately, as all Oakland schools were closed for the duration of the flu epidemic. I'd read the article about schools closing in the Oakland paper that said: "It is widely believed that the Bolsheviks have released the flu bugs into our country."

Bolsheviks, I decided, couldn't be that bad if they prevented me from starting another new school.

Growing Up in a Changing World
1921–1926

SATURDAYS!—A CLUSTER OF many Saturdays—I waited at the employees' door for Mother, who worked in the basement of Capwell's Department Store for three dollars a day. I spent most Saturday afternoons at a matinee at the nearby American Theater. There was sure to be a "kid's show" with either a Mary Pickford film, a Charlie Chaplin comedy, or a western. Most theaters attempted to please parents by advertising movies as "suitable for children," for Saturday matinees.

At other showings the movie producers' advertisements left little doubt about the moral revolution in the country: *Petting Parties in Motor Cars, Kisses to Make You Gasp, Naked Truth of Champagne Baths, Sensational Hot Love-Making,* etc.

In response to a storm of protest from the church organizations and women's groups, motion-picture producers engaged Will H. Hays, President Harding's postmaster general, to censor the morals and good taste of their products. In a speech to the Los Angeles Chamber of Commerce, Mr. Hays spoke of "that sacred thing, the mind of a child" and demanded that the entertainment industry take the same responsibility as the most inspired clergyman "toward that clean virgin thing, that unmarked slate."

The producers responded with pious remarks and continued to release movies that people lined up around the block to see. The marquees displayed such titles as: *Flames of the Flesh, The She-Tiger, The Sin-Sister,* and *Girls Gone Wild.*

I can remember but few violent movies. There was shooting and chasing in *The Automobile Thieves* and *The Great American Train Robbery*, but killing never seemed any more real in these movies than in the westerns.

The McDonald sisters discussed "the awful way things are changing." They whispered when the cousins were present.

During morning hours before the matinee, I sat on the mezzanine floor of Capwell's Department Store and looked in the forbidden movie magazines and a *True Confessions* for stories with the word "sex" in the title. I'd been taught that nice girls didn't even think about such things until they were married. I guessed that nice girls didn't have my curiosity. Sometimes I'd observe shoppers on the floor below. Bobbed hair was no longer considered a badge of prostitution. Teenagers in their sassy short skirts intrigued me, especially a group at the cosmetic counter. They were trying on lipstick, which had become acceptable. Rouge was still seen only on "that kind of woman."

Beneath the store's high dome, fragrance from the cosmetic department mingled with stuffy odors of people, artificial lights, leather, and food from the lunch room. At noon I joined Mother in the employees' cafeteria where I marveled at the selection of desserts. After lunch I was off for the matinee, proud of the quarter in my small purse. The theater was only a couple of blocks from Capwell's store, and I felt grown-up and happy on my own.

I kept no happy memories of the long wait for Mother at the employees' entrance. Each time the door opened I looked down the dark stairway at women plodding up from the basement. Required to wear black, they approached with the weary clop-clop-clop of Cuban heels on metal stairs. At the top of the stair, the rhythm broke as each woman punched a time clock, proof that she'd earned her three dollars for eight hours. If Dad's theory that we perform best when we move to an inner rhythm was true, then apparently some activities required a dirge. Tired faces filed past me and I searched each for the one who could quicken the beat of my heart. Sometimes I liked to scare myself by pretending Mom wouldn't come, so as to experience the glad relief at her appearance.

An icy wind whipped around the corner of E. 14th and Broadway where Mom and I waited for the street car.

～

What did Mother ever do for fun? Sometimes she went to a Sunday matinee with me. Dad never cared for movies, so he would be reading a book, building a birdbath or off to the sloughs on a fishing trip with his buddies. Usually Mother needed Sundays "to catch up": a day for ironing my school dresses and Dad's blue shirts, for mending and cooking.

Often Dad suggested she stay home and "take it easy, Tereda." She seldom answered.

"Since you had some money for a change," she might retort, "why couldn't you have bought us a decent home?"

"And let those loan sharks feed on us? If we live within our means, the little Turk here can go to college."

"You needn't worry—I've saved for that."

More school! Would I ever be through with it?

～

"The streetcar should be along in twenty minutes or so." Mother shivered in her thin coat.

That twenty minutes seemed longer than when I waited for the recess bell. I knew when Mom's feet hurt because the fine lines around her mouth deepened. Then I watched for a place on the bench so I could slide in quickly and save it for her.

At last the streetcar came, then it took forty-five minutes—stopping at every second block—to reach Harrington Avenue. Out again into the chilly evening we started that long walk between the shacks to reach the last one in the row, 2088 Harrington Ave.

Dad called the house "our little nest." Mom referred to "The Pillboxes." These homes, built on narrow lots, huddled together like a crowd in a disaster. The back lots climbed a steep bank, yellow with weeds. Some of the owners, perhaps in a desperate effort to escape anonymity, resorted to color.

Mom and I played a game to shorten our walk.

"Here's the Blueing Bottle House," I would chant.

Mom's tired smile appeared and she responded, "Next comes the Three Gray Mice followed by Shanty Irish Green."

"And here's Pumpkin, Pumpkin." I would start to giggle waiting for Mom's wicked name for the next house.

"Ah ha," she replied, "my favorite—Baby Shit Brown."

We'd laugh together and being poor didn't matter.

We passed small yards, where neglected lawns and weeds displayed the broken and discarded: doll carts, baby buggies, an old Ford tire. Groups of screaming, laughing children played Kick the Can or One Foot Off the Gutter. I greeted Etta and Ellen Lyons, girls around my age, whom I played with at times. Somewhere babies were forever crying. Usually it was around the dinner hour when Mom and I headed home, and smells of cabbage, turnips, fish, or burned carrots drifted from doorways.

Nearly home, we passed the one tree, a plum with a few red leaves, small buds swelling on fragile branches.

"Someday," Mother would promise wistfully, "you will live a different life. You'll have a lovely home and won't even remember living here."

It seemed she was always saying things like that.

Finally we reach our gray "nest." Dad kept the lawn, the size of a post card, mowed. Mom had planted a border of bright marigolds.

It must have been fall of 1920 when the flu epidemic subsided and I, ten years old, enrolled at Jefferson School. With clothes slightly outgrown from Cleveland School, I blended into the background without being different. But I was never comfortable.

On weekdays, I was a latchkey kid. While Mom worked, Dad, after his hours on the swing shift, slept. So I need not disturb him, Mom hid the house key under an obvious flower pot on the front porch saying, "A burglar would take one look at this joint and snort."

By then, I'd decided not to give the kids at school a chance to snort. Cleveland School left me sharply aware of social class. Since Mother thought it disgraceful to live on Harrington Avenue, I kept my address a secret from my classmates. I resorted to circuitous ways to go home, usually concluded by scrambling and sliding down the back bank to the house with no thought of those freshly ironed school dresses. If I made no friends, I would have no guests.

Dad did not hesitate to invite friends. The first time, I was surprised when a big Willys Knight drove up in front of our house on a Sunday. Mom rushed around gathering up newspapers and puffing pillows. Dad stopped in the midst of shaving to go to the door. With his suspenders over his B.V.D.'s, he greeted his wealthy friend heartily. They shared glasses of wine and talked of the growing fear of bomb explosions by radicals and of Woodrow Wilson's failure in Paris to sell the League of Nations.

"Elmer has no sense of what's fitting," Mom said.

It puzzled me. Dad seemed happy on Harrington Avenue. Not as happy as in our mountain cabin, but content. And everyone appeared to like him. If he wasn't ashamed of our house, why should Mom and I be? I wished I could be like Dad, but I recognized my leanings toward Mom.

At home I would warm up the chocolate that waited in a saucepan on the stove and look in the cookie jar for the two surprise doughnuts or cookies. Two, because Mother expected I might bring "a little friend" home. Mom always left a note to greet me.

"But don't ever bring boys in the house when you're alone,"

she would remind me. "And don't ever let a boy kiss you. Boys are different from girls. Once they start, they can't stop."

I wasn't certain what she was talking about. Out of the school-room, my nearest proximity to males occurred during gym classes when boys played ball on one side of the school yard while I, in my long gym bloomers that covered the tops of black cotton hosiery, played girls' volleyball on the other side. I could hardly be mistaken for one of the cast in *Girls Gone Wild*.

Our tiny house, even with Dad sleeping out back on the closed-in porch, seemed hollow at times. I had the solitude that I'd longed for over the past years since we left the mountains, and I had Snowball and Truce. But I didn't have The Sandy Shore, the music of the river, and the security of knowing a large and loving family surrounded me in the nearby prairie or woods.

When I wanted playmates I joined the Lyons girls on our block. More often I stayed in, to write stories on the breakfast-nook table. Somewhere between the ages of nine and ten, I had forsaken The Wad for the pencil. It was likely around the same time when I man-aged to get words down without concentrating on the process.

The stories I wrote, probably influenced by the current movies, became romances. In the sixth grade whatever literary leanings I might have had faded with the awakening of the sensorium. I wrote a series of Emma and Earl Stories. Emma, the prettiest girl in sixth grade had auburn curls, brown eyes, and a short nose with a blunt tip. Earl must have been a Scandinavian boy with his fair hair, deep blue eyes, and tanned skin. The two appeared to be inseparable, sit-ting together in the library to study, walking about hand-in-hand at recess, and wandering away after school with Earl carrying Emma's books and lunch box. This romance moved me to sighs.

The stories these two inspired I could never show to the teacher. I related my fantasies to Helen on the Friday nights I spent with her after we had been to a musical show.

The general plot involved Emma and Earl being kidnapped by evil men.

"These men made them do bad things to each other," I whispered to Helen after we were in bed. Then I would direct her to act a part in this lurid melodrama.

It was by far the most intriguing game we'd ever played. We took turns being Emma or Earl.

I instructed her on the necessity of showing great reluctance for the betrayal of feminine modesty before lifting small nightgowns to gaze at each other. Each of us being an only child, we missed the early thrill of playing doctor games. It was a necessary part of the plot that the two friends be forced into this performance by wicked men. I found this game so exciting that I often wondered if I was turning out to be one of those modern "bad girls" my mother and her sisters were always talking about.

By this time a love for dancing equalled my joy in writing. Sometimes I became a leaf in the wind, sometimes a robin or a great, swooping hawk. I danced to music that I had heard in dancing school, usually Tchaikovsky or Chopin.

My fantasy life and dance training merged. I became obsessed—as all dancers do—with my body as an instrument and soon forgot the Emma-Earl games. Aunt Kitty took Helen and me to a weekly ballet class. Our dancing teacher played a Chopin work that made me believe—briefly—that I was a swan. Discovering I could play-act with my body became such a delight that the Harrington house and friendless days at school no longer mattered. As I'd discovered long ago, the best things that could happen took place within the head, an interior stage with no limits. I watched leading pupils in the class and studied my teacher in motion. Everything within me responded to the beauty of a body so disciplined it could break with gravity and sail off into music. I vowed to practice ballet barre daily, to remake bones and muscles, to reshape a vehicle to interpret my vision.

But the material world has a way of intruding on dreams when they are within sight.

On the day of my twelfth birthday Dad became sick. I panicked when the doctor came. Dad stayed home from the shipyards for many weeks. After Mother said it was his heart, I worried daily that he would die. Without his salary, we had less meat, no ballet class, and on Saturdays I stayed with the Dunnings instead of going to the matinee.

The only good thing was having Dad's companionship when I returned from school. As he grew stronger we took long walks. Dad must have noticed that I never brought friends home, for once he told me that I must not be afraid of being different. Most people, he explained, tried to be alike—to live in the same kind of house and wear "the same duds." It was being different that made you interesting.

I wondered if he was right.

Moving Up

ONE DAY I HEARD Mother tell Aunt Agnes, "Elmer needs a white-collar job. The shipyards are too hard on him. I'm going to see Will Hodges. It's time he did something for his brother-in-law."

I hoped it would be a job Dad didn't hate. Maybe Mom wouldn't have to work so hard. The time chosen by Mother to confront her difficult brother-in-law appeared to be a propitious one.

In 1924, jobs were plentiful, but for men younger than Dad; he had passed sixty that year. However, most of the employees in the Alameda County Tax Office, including Dad's brother-in-law William Hodges, were around Dad's age. The Harding presidency introduced an era of prosperity. With plentiful work, people reached for all the toys they'd been denied in the war years: automobiles, new homes, phonographs, clothes, and gadgets.

The very idea of anyone asking favors of Uncle William Hodges was unimaginable to me. I called him Uncle William so as not to confuse him with Uncle Will Dunning. Besides, Uncle William suited him. If Mother had announced she was going to interview old Scrooge, I could not have been more intimidated for her. Years later when I published my first children's book, *Mystery of the Swan Ballet*, I took the characters from my father's sister, Minnie (Pedlar) Hodges, and her half-sister, Etta. Aunt Minnie, badly crippled with arthritis, spent her days in a wheelchair and suffered great difficulty in even trying to get a spoon to her mouth. Aunt Etta cared for her.

These relatives of my father lived in Alameda. I found it easy to write of a child's reaction to that big, gloomy house. Mother dreaded going there and I shared her feelings. Minnie and Will had three daughters, Norma, Henrietta, and the youngest, Myra—who died in childbirth.

We were visiting on the day Minnie heard the news of her daughter's death. Aunt Minnie's sorrow reached down into me when Etta stood nearby to wipe her tears. My emotion that day preserved details of that house of grief.

William Hodges, a taciturn man, wore that grief like an unremovable mask. Being too young to understand his bitterness, I found him cross and forbidding. Dad appeared to be the only one who could evoke Uncle William's strange laugh, a laugh that shook his big body for a moment without a sound. He liked Dad and accompanied him on fishing trips.

William was Assistant Tax Collector under his good friend, Edward Planer.

~~~~~~

While Mother told Agnes her intentions to get a job for Dad in the tax office, I listened with fear. We were sitting in Agnes's brand new 1924 Chevrolet coupe and the conversation went something like this:

"Oh Tess!" Agnes would cry. "Without letting Elmer know what you're going to do? How could you even think of it?"

Aunt Agnes didn't know that my parents never considered discussing important decisions until the deed was done. It was a pattern. For them, communication appeared to be a challenge on the same level as attempting to decipher the Dead Sea Scrolls.

"When do you plan to see Mr. Hodges?" Agnes turned to Mother, blue eyes attentive."Will you go to his house?"

I trembled. But Mother seemed to thrive on difficult situations. Would Uncle William thunder refusal?

"I'll go down to the tax office," Mother replied to her sister. "He can take me to lunch."

Later I heard the results of this interview played back to Aunt Agnes. Mother's words, repeated to each of her sisters, are etched on my mind, perhaps by emotion. Our future, including ballet lessons, balanced on tiptoe.

Uncle Will had told my mother it was out of the question. "He said that Elmer would have to take the Civil Service Examination. 'I know that, Will,' I informed him. 'Elmer is bright. He'll pass.'"

Then, according to Mother, Will had told her that Elmer would hate a desk job; that she was doing him no favor by trying to run his life—

"Well," Mother exclaimed, "I put an end to that! 'William Hodges,' I said, 'I don't give a fig what Elmer likes or doesn't like, or for that matter—what you like!' I was mad, and I told him, 'I have a daughter to think of and it's time you did something for your brother-in-law's family!'"

"Poor William," my Aunt put in, laughing. "He might know he didn't have a chance once your mind was made up, Tess."

Mother smiled with satisfaction. Then she informed Agnes that Will had arranged for Elmer to take the Civil Service Exam. There was a possibility, she added, that we might get Will's old car later.

That was when she uttered these amazing words: "Now, I want you to list the Harrington Avenue shack, Agnes, and find us something we can afford in an acceptable home."

My Aunt focused an amazed stare on Mom. "Without telling Ped, I suspect?"

That year Agnes had opened her own real estate office in her home in east Oakland; Wells Realtor later became Wells and Bennett. Big parcels of vacant land, in those years, were being divided into lots for homes and office buildings. Hardly a week went by without an invitation for lunch or picnic from some realtor with a house or lot to sell in East Oakland or "country land" in nearby Orinda. My aunt did well in the real estate business.

Dad did well, too. He passed the examination as Mom knew he would. He appeared amused, not annoyed, at Mother for getting him a job. I believe William was wrong about Dad not wanting a desk job. At that time. Dad must have realized he was too old for labor and, although he protested every time he put on that stiff collar, I believe he was relieved to have the job.

In May 1925, Mom pulled her second surprise. We went to look at a house in East Oakland on Coolidge Avenue.

The tan house occupied one story over a basement. I went at once to check on the bathroom. It opened discreetly on a hall between the two bedrooms. The sunny kitchen looked out on a large yard with two trees, an apple and a cherry. The Coolidge Avenue house would put us well ahead of The Poor, yet modestly behind The Rich. I remember this scene as if I'd rehearsed it.

"Well," Mother announced, as she swept like a duchess through a long living room with a fireplace at the far end, "I hope you like it because I bought it."

Dad whirled around to stare at her while I chewed a thumb nail. "Where did you get the money? Why couldn't you at least have waited until our house was sold—"

"It is sold. The cash made a down payment on this."

Then her manner softened and she sent a hesitant glance from me to Dad. "Well, what do you think of it?"

I nodded and held my breath. Dad appeared thoughtful for a moment, then shook his head with that laughing expression that asks me, "What will she do next?"

"Tereda," he replied, "I've always known you'd never be satisfied 'til you had glass knobs on the toilet door."

"Now," Mother turned to me. "You need never be ashamed to entertain your friends." She added something about managing the move in good time—before I started high school that fall.

She managed it. It must have taken nearly all of the 15 years since I was born.

That day, I believe Dad gave in to Mom's ways. Reluctantly he agreed to charge accounts as everyone we knew was buying on credit, although he never stopped his angry protests when the bills came.

The Coolidge Avenue home was about thirty years old when we moved in. An iron wood-burning stove with a water heater warmed the kitchen on cold mornings while we ate in the adjoining breakfast room. In the rear a small laundry held the added luxury of a cold box, filled weekly by an ice man. A rear door led to a large garden where Dad put up a hammock under the apple tree. Later he experimented on grafting a fig tree onto the cherry. We'd traveled a great distance from the cabin in The Divide. It must have given Mom satisfaction to have achieved the goal for which she'd worked for so long. My parents quarreled less and less after we moved into the house on Coolidge. With Dad earning the magnificent salary of $200 a month, Mom stayed home and discovered she had the "green thumb." I returned to dance classes.

During that summer, William Hodges bought a new car and Dad acquired William's 1919 Jordan Touring Car. Dad wasted no time in planning weekend fishing trips and I think he lived for those weekends when he would load up the old Jordan with camping gear and head for the Mokelumne or Stanislaus River. I don't remember Mother coming with us. Usually she'd spend that time in the city with one or more of her sisters. But I went with Dad, who helped me perfect the fly fishing he'd taught me in Bull Run. Sometimes Dad asked one of his brothers-in-law or our neighbors, the Riis boys; often he and I went alone. Once out of the city he would sing and, at night, around the campfire, he became the story teller. I like to remember those warm evenings in the mountain air with the glow from the campfire flickering on faces while Dad entertained from his fund of tales.

My story-telling days were crowded out. As I neared sixteen, I took a part-time job in order to pay for ballet lessons. This job involved giving out free samples from a bakery in the newly organized Independent Stores. These smaller "Ma and Pa Stores" had formed a union in California to try to keep from being squeezed out of business by the growing chain stores, such as Piggly Wiggly and the U.P. stores.

Dad felt certain the independents would never succeed. Our grocer, Mr. Callari, confided in Dad that his business was in jeopardy. He could no longer afford to deliver groceries since the chain stores were undercutting his prices.

Dad became inflamed at such injustice. I was exposed to much rhetoric concerning monopolies and antitrust laws. Dad pointed out that it was happening in many businesses, such as theaters, clothing stores, and gas stations.

"No one protects the little guy anymore. Our world is changing rapidly," he would say. "You'll never see the same times again, Little Turk."

It was a subject that worried him. Even on the first day of high school, when Dad drove me to school, he told me that we were beginning to lose the free-enterprise system on which this country was built. He felt that if something was not done to stop the greed, the nation would keep sliding downhill. "You may live to see the fall of America."

I would have preferred that Dad didn't drive me to school, but I didn't want to hurt his feelings. I feared I might look like a rich snob. My ideas of wealth were shaped by the contrast of what we'd known. It would take time to grow accustomed to moving up in the world.

As we neared Roosevelt High School on that first day, Dad finally turned from politics to recite from the *Rubaiyat*:

> *Yet ah, that spring should vanish with the rose!*
> *That Youth's sweet-scented manuscript should close!*
> *The Nightingale that in the branches sang,*
> *Ah, whence, and whither flown again, who knows!*

I was fearful of a new school where, as always, I would be forced to recognize the differences that set me apart from my

classmates. It had never been possible for me to be at home in the
people-world as Dad was.

But at Roosevelt High something different happened. Miss
Rayburn, the gym teacher, organized a dance class. One morning
she chose me, along with two other girls, to dance in the school
festival. I couldn't believe it! Soon these girls became my friends.

"You shall be the three flowers," Miss Rayburn said. "Flower of
lily, flower of rose, and flower of columbine—as the poem goes."

"The rose is a perfect part for you," said Eve, the lily. "I wish I
had a skin that reminded people of roses, instead of yellow onions!"

With Eve for a chum, my grades went from C's to A's. Slowly
I gained in confidence although I continued to suffer shyness
through those school years.

Eve matched me in height: five-foot-seven. Far more attractive
than prettier girls, she had a beckoning curve to her lips like a
model on a magazine cover. Her smile revealed baby teeth, short,
evenly spaced, and white as angel cake. Blond hair curled in a sassy
windblown bob. When she danced the Charleston, her skirts flew
up to reveal skin above her rolled stockings. At school she was
called "Speedy." I was "Peaches."

Both new friends assured me I was pretty. I began to look in
mirrors and take pleasure in curly brown hair while I tried to con-
tort a round, babyish face into expressing sophistication. I longed
to project a more jazzy image than "Peaches" for it was "Speedy"
who got the dates.

That year Eve and I enrolled in ballet classes in San Francisco.
My dancing dreams set sail.

After graduating from Roosevelt High School, Eve and I joined
Fanchon and Marco, a theatrical company, and traveled around
the United States dancing as a sister team.

When I returned home in 1934 to be married and to open a dance studio, I found my parents more content than I had ever seen them. Dad continued to take the old Jordan for weekend camping trips. Mom spent more time with her sisters: days for lunch or shopping in San Francisco. Mom and Dad gardened together and often played auction bridge with the neighbors.

One day in September 1935, my Aunt Mary came into the dance studio while I was teaching a ballet class. She called me aside and told me my father was dying. I dismissed the class and went with her to the Coolidge Avenue house. Many of Mom's family were lined up in the hallway waiting their turn to say goodbye. They parted to let me through.

"Dad?" I took his hand to rub my thumb over the stumps of his fingers.

He opened his eyes. "Little Turk."

He did not speak again. I was glad he had lived long enough to see me enrolled in the University of California Extension Division and embarked on a writing career.

Mom enjoyed her two grandchildren and lived until 1965 when, at eighty-five, she became a great grandmother.

Epilogue

It WAS NOT UNTIL 1986 that I returned with my son, Gary, to northeastern Nevada. I was searching for my childhood. Without parental help, the earliest years of one's life are most difficult to piece together. Although I might guess at Mother's reluctance to speak of Nevada, I was never certain of the reason. On the rare occasions when Dad reminisced, Mom's thin lips would all but disappear.

When I arrived at the Elko Courthouse to began the search, I was prepared for disappointment as anyone pursuing ephemeral memories into a distant past should be.

But there was nothing ephemeral about these records. Here were Dad's mines: the Aganini, the Tereda, and the Turk Quartz— duly recorded in a massive, dusty ledger.

Signatures of both parents were in that ledger. And there is something startlingly intimate about seeing a familiar signature after many years: after decades it's like a sudden appearance of a ghost. I ran my fingers lightly over my father's fine penmanship, which made a statement for his literacy. Beneath it, as witness to the three claims, Mother's signature made up in bold and determined strokes for what she lacked in training. Hers was a brave signature.

From the courthouse, we walked down Main Street to the Elko Museum. From the moment I put time in reverse surprising events occurred: there, at the museum, I met Antoine Primeaux, my friend from the first grade in Tuscarora! He, another writer, was engaged in researching a history of that ghost town.

He helped me locate old newspapers at the museum where I began to connect with a few events. In an August paper of 1917, a small item caught my attention. It told of a landslide on the Bull Run Mine. Antoine had been in first grade when I registered at the one-room schoolhouse in Tuscarora so we knew I was in Tuscarora that late summer of 1917. Another item, copied from a Tuscarora paper, uncovered missing parts of the puzzle; my father, Elmer Pedlar, was hired as foreman to rescue the Bull Run Mine following a landslide. By then, the retrieve keys were bringing up lost feelings, pieces, people, and spoken words. It was almost too much. Antoine spoke to me and I was unable to answer. He offered to drive us over Mount Blitzen and to help me locate the site of my former home at The Divide.

As Antoine drove his jeep up that road, narrow and treacherous as a rattler, the hot August air mingled with a familiar smell of sage, bringing back a river scene, the first of many lost memories. I suppose most children grow up hearing stories of early childhood. This sharing of memories weaves security into the very rug beneath the feet of a family. To reach adulthood without such information is like floundering for directions in a foreign land. It helps to have a guide with a map: "Look, you have been here. And here. This is the road you have traveled to arrive where you are now."

I looked down at the map of northeastern Nevada. By running my finger up the road, I discovered the small print—The Divide. Yes, I have been here.

The jeep bounced like a cow-puncher's horse over bumpy terrain, over sheep brush and sage brush, over a few wild flowers—yellow mules-ears and blue lupin. We explored dirt roads, then deserted all roads to cross a dried creek bed. All the while, I kept looking for the mountain with the zig-zag trail; the mountain that would help me find the place where once a small cabin squeezed in between the slope and Jack's Creek.

We located Jack's Creek but the mountains receded as we approached them. While we traveled across a long stretch of hot, dusty field, myriads of locust gave the ground an appearance of quivering beneath the car.

Antoine pointed out where Barney Horn's Saloon and Post Office once stood at The Divide. He followed the dry bed of Jack's Creek North. Then he made a turn toward the mountain and—

"There it is! Our cabin!" I cried, not really believing it.

"It could be another cabin built since—" Antoine started to warn me while he stopped alongside the creek bed.

For a few moments we remained in the car looking in disbelief at the sagging log cabin with the tin roof. It seemed impossible that our cabin could still be standing. Then I raised my eyes knowing exactly where the outhouse should be and there it was. This was our cabin. I knew before we went inside to find clues of my family: a tricycle part, rusty springs from my old cot in the lean-to, boxes with California labels—part of a torn label read City Of Paris. Stacks of magazines we had once subscribed to, damp and stuck together, proved to be *St. Nicholas, Saturday Evening Post* and *Ladies Home Journal.* I felt disoriented.

The cabin, with its tin-can roof and weathered log siding, looked as if it might sail away on the next strong wind. Part of the floor was gone but enough remained for me to see the spaces between wall and floor and I shivered, half expecting a reptile head to slither up.

From the doorway I found landmarks I'd been looking for: the dry creek bed in front of the cabin, a cluster of cottonwood trees that may have shaded The Sandy Shore. The mountain in the rear was not as high as it once appeared to a five-year-old, and gone was any trace of a zig-zag trail. Gone, too, was the house on the summit.

But even more moving than what I saw from the cabin door that day was the strange feeling brought on by mountain silence to stir memory. It was difficult to believe there could be a place in the world where there was no radio, automobile, or human sounds, only an occasional bird or cricket. Memories rushed into that remembered silence in a different way: I relived bits of scenes as Mom and Dad's voices, still preserved here where I'd heard them long ago, spoke to each other in familiar phrases. Directed by my parent's words, I traveled both forward and backward in time.

～

Now in 1995 I am on top of that mountain again, a place to look down, not only on Tuscarora town where there was no room for storytellers, but on a vista that has widened to reach clear across the twentieth century. At 85, it appears I missed only a decade at the beginning of this century and may miss a snippet at the end. Looking back across the years, I hear the clop-clop of horses' feet on dirt roads, then sounds change to spluttering motors and auto horns, accelerating as speed increases and the poisonous smog rises higher and higher over freeways.

Yet here, high on The Divide, I have always believed that nothing ever changes. Here the young deer follow their parents nibbling the sweet spring grass on the hillsides; here the beaver continue to build dams in the river near the aspen forest; here rainbow trout hide in the shadows by the bank while all the endless possibilities of Never-Never Land hover above The Sandy Shore. Silent with the clean smell of mountain air, impervious to time and change, nature waits out the "war to end wars"—and the treaties and wars to follow. From my mountain top, I can see decades of discovery: science and technology improving human lives—providing new wonders in health, music, entertainment, and exploring deeper than ever before the mysteries of existence. Yet from this vista, flaws rise like mushroom clouds to darken patches of racing time. Every decline in creativity with its built-in spiritual values is counterbalanced by increase in greed. The technology that gave us spinning wheels and wings left violence in men's hearts and the most destructive of weapons in their hands.

Now, in 1995, on my last visit to The Divide, I am saddened by the knowledge that nature is no longer impervious to the shenanigans of mankind. I recognize the pollution in the rivers. I miss the quick movement of the rainbow trout in the leafy shadows of the water. Where have the deer gone, and the beaver? What has happened to the plethora of rabbits, squirrels, and chipmunks? Forests have vanished, taking with them the clean smell of mountain air and sage.

The smell of sage returns as it did on that hot August day, driving back down Mount Blitzen to Tuscarora, the day I decided to write the book. Allured, not only by the memories that shone like glow worms in a black cavern, but also by the myriad of events unlit in the dark, I knew I wanted to follow the trail back through the lost landscape of my childhood. Was it possible, using concentration as a tool, to dig deeply enough to unearth a fresh layer of recall? Would my parents continue to speak to me in those well-remembered phrases? In my mother's voice I could hear her bitterness: her shame over our poverty, our isolation, and, of course, The Wad.

But only now that the book is finished, the irony of the situation becomes apparent: the realization that my parents, who will never know, gave me the greatest possible gift—the gift of solitude within the realm of nature, a place in the world that reflects a place within. In that setting I found creativity.

Sometimes my thoughts transport me to the river's edge where I once summoned the storyteller, waving not a wand, but The Wad. For it is here with the sand warm beneath me, with river secrets murmuring in my ears, with the smell of sage and the distant cry of a wolf, where my storyteller's voice speaks again.

Index

Aganini Mine, 42, 46, 188
Alameda County Tax Office, Hodges at,
    180
American Theater, matinees at, 172
Animals
    learning about, 11–12, 14–16, 67, 68–69
    love for, 5, 16–17, 21, 22
Armistice, celebrating, 162–165
Automobile ride, first, 114

Bad language, story about, 37
Beavers, learning about, 68–69
Berkeley, living in, 122–136
Billings (labor leader), 120–121
Birthday party, 95, 98
Black Beauty (Sewell), 89
Boarders, 95, 96
Boarding house, 63, 80, 94–96
    cooking at, 60, 61
Bolsheviks, 62, 90, 120, 151–152, 171
Bond drive, 103, 104, 105, 127
Books, 71, 72, 89
Borax Smith estate, 148
Brewery Saloon, 35
Briggs, Mrs., 93
Buck Horn's Saloon and Post Office, 4,
    44, 51, 190
Bull Run Mining District, 75, 116, 189
    living in, 64, 65–74
Bull Run River, 7, 33, 65, 67–68, 74
Bull Run Saloon, 70
Burke, Katherine, 140–143
    murders and, 144–145
Burke, Louise, 141
    murder of, 144

Burke, Rainey, 140, 142, 145
    murder of, 144
Burke, Robert: murder by, 144
Burke Funeral Home, 138
Butcher Shop, 38

Cabin, 4–5, 21, 24
    finding, 190–191
Cabinet Saloon, 34
Calico (cat), 61, 66, 67, 77, 86, 100
California
    returning to, 108–112
    stories about, 41
California Fruit Growers Supply Com-
    pany, 117
Callari, Mr., 185
Cally (bully), 149–150, 152, 153
Camp cookies. *See* Hardtack
Capwell's Department Store, Mother at,
    170, 172, 173–174
Carson River, 33
Cassatt, Mary, 130
Castle, Irene, 102, 140
Celerity wagon. *See* Mud wagon
Chaplin, Charlie, 172
Childhood
    enchanted, 10–11
    searching for, 188–192
Child's Companion, 72
China (dishes), 95–96, 98
Chinese, 35, 58
Chinese Wash House, 35, 38
Chipmunks, 67, 73, 171
Chocolate, 39, 52, 176
Christian Science, 130–131

Christmas, 80, 88–89, 167
City of Paris store, 57, 60, 128, 132, 190
Civil Service Examination, Dad and, 182–183
Cleveland School, 146
  attending, 148, 149–153, 155, 159
Clothes, school, 57–59, 61, 89, 159, 175–176
Coffee Dan's, 115
Columbia Mine, Dad at, 64, 66
Commission of Immigration and Housing, inspection by, 120
Composition, patriotism, 103–105
Cooking, 5, 13, 60, 61, 88
Coolidge Avenue, house on, 183–187
Cowan, Miss, 107
  patriotism composition and, 104–105
Crawford, Brandy, 49, 50

Daily Free Press, 62
Dancing, 118, 128–129, 140–141, 178, 184, 186, 187
"Dangerous Dan McGrew," 35, 59
Death, awareness of, 138, 142, 144–145
DeFrees Mine, 34
Delta Saloon, 35
Dentists, 78–79
Dexter's Mill, 33, 44
Divide Mining District, 7, 49–50, 54, 67, 73, 110, 116, 189, 190
  leaving, 64
  problems in, 21
  return to, 192
Dolls, 86, 89
Dolly (horse), 4, 23, 34, 64, 76, 114
  accident involving, 47–49, 50–51
Duck Valley Indian Reservation, 13
Dunning, Helen, 121, 122, 135, 139, 140, 145, 146, 150, 155, 157
  Christmas with, 167
  dancing with, 128, 178
  described, 123
  dinner party and, 134
  Emma and Earl Stories and, 178
  Flying Circus and, 153
  ice box accident and, 128
  quarrel with, 147

singing by, 126
vision problems for, 130–131
Dunning, Katherine McDonald "Kitty," 12, 41, 71–72, 121, 123–125, 130
  Christmas with, 167
  on Dad, 159
  dancing lessons and, 178
  dinner party and, 131, 134, 135
  dressmaking by, 132–134
  flu epidemic and, 150
  Flying Circus and, 153
  ice box accident and, 128–129
  letters from, 71
  living with, 125–126, 145
  separation for, 146, 147, 157
  on Mother, 128
  songs by, 126
Dunning, Will, 41, 71–72, 121, 123, 126, 127, 129, 133–135, 180
  car of, 122
  described, 124–125
  separation for, 146, 147, 157

Eagle Drop Stage Stop, 87
Eagle Rock, 3
Education. *See* School
Elephant Mobile, 8
Elko, 3
  traveling to, 86, 88
Elko Courthouse, 1, 188
Elko Grammar School, bond drive at, 103
Elko High School, 94
Elko Hospital, 88, 89–90, 91, 94
Elko Independent, 81–82, 85, 86, 91
Elko Museum, 188
Ellen May (childhood acquaintance), 92
Ellie, Aunt, 132, 146
Emma and Earl Stories, acting out, 177–178
End of the Trail, The (painting), 139, 143
Erasmus, 105, 106, 107
  on war, 104
Eve (dance class), 186

Fairy Tales (Grimms), 6
Fall of the Nation, The, 90, 102, 103
Fanchon (dancer), 132, 133, 134

Fanchon and Marco Revue, 126, 127–128
  joining, 186
Ferry Building, 127, 137
Fields, Mrs., 95, 96
First Avenue, memories of, 147–148
Fishing, 8, 9, 10, 23, 25, 65, 74, 174, 184
Flu epidemic, 107, 110, 136, 137, 147, 150, 160, 162-164, 171, 175–176
Flying Circus air show, 153–154, 155
Fourth of July, celebrating, 62–63
Free-enterprise system, Dad on, 185
Frisky (chipmunk), 67, 161
Fritz (squirrel), shooting of, 25
Front Street, 34
  Chinese on, 35
Fruitvale, home in, 167–171
Funeral game, 137–145

Gem Restaurant, The (Chinese restaurant), 35, 52
Girl of the Limberlost (Porter), 67, 90
God, questions about, 11
Gold, 45–46
  liquid, 111, 112
  panning for, 42–43
Goshute Indians, 7
Gramophone, 139, 140, 142
Grand Prize Mine, bullion from, 3
Grange, 117, 120
Grocery stores, 52, 184–185

Hacker, Gary, 188
Hardtack, 26, 28, 38
Harrington Avenue, living on, 172–179
Hawkins, Pastor, 62
Hays, Will H.: censorship by, 172
Heidi, 22, 67, 116
Heiner, Miss, 151
  composition for, 152–153, 155
  described, 148–149
  petticoat incident and, 156
  story for, 150
Herbert, Victor, 90
Hi Li, laundry by, 35
"Hinky Dinky Parlez Vous," 126, 164
Hodges, Henrietta, 181
Hodges, Minnie Pedlar, 19, 71, 180
  described, 181

Hodges, Myra, 181
Hodges, Norma, 181
Hodges, William, 71, 183
  car of, 184
  described, 181
  Mom interview with, 180, 182
Home remedies, using, 79
Horn, Barney, 62, 84
Horn, Buck, 25, 35–36, 49, 61, 62, 77–78, 83, 84
  bad language and, 37
Hospital, 88, 89–90, 91
  working at, 85, 94
House naming, 174
Huddleson (Dad's partner), 5, 23, 27, 46, 76, 100
Humboldt National Forest, 65
Humboldt Sink, 7
Huns, 12, 47, 62, 72, 104
Hunting, 25
  exposure to, 15–16, 17

Ice box, accident involving, 128–129
Idaho Saloon, 35
Independence Mountain, 75
  mines on, 42
Independent Stores, job at, 184–185
Indians and immigrants (game), playing, 91–92
Industrial Workers of the World (I.W.W.), 121, 134
  at Wheatland Ranch, 119–120
Industry, expansion of, 114, 117

Jack's Creek, 7, 13, 29, 68, 189, 190
Jefferson School, 171
  attending, 175–176
Jerky (horse), 4, 23, 34
Johnson School of Classical and Skirt Dancing for Young Misses, attending, 128, 140–141
Jordan Touring Car, 184, 187
Joss House, 35
Jung, Carl, 9

Keeper of the Bees, The (Porter), 67
Kittens, 52, 53, 54, 116, 117, 123
  disembobulated, 165–166

Ladies' Home Journal, 72, 190
La Marr, Dora, 52–57, 61, 78, 79, 83, 84
Lamoile, rabbit drive at, 106
Lee, Charles Frederick, 154
Lehnharts, 132
Liberty Bonds, 103, 104, 105, 127
Liquid gold, 111, 112
Little, Mrs., 88, 90, 91, 94, 102
Littlefield, Mrs. C. J.: hospital and, 85
"Little Nemo" cartoon, 81, 104
London, Jack, 72, 81
Loneliness, 70, 118, 129
Lone Mt. Station, 87
Long Tom, 45, 46
Lying, problems with, 108–109
Lyons, Ellen, 175, 177
Lyons, Etta, 175, 177

McDonald, Bessie, 71, 132, 146
McDonald, Bob, 71
McDonald, Laughlin, 18, 131
McDonald, Lockie, 71
McDonald, Mary, 137, 187
    books from, 71, 89
    letters from, 71
McDonald clan, 4, 7, 124, 173
Magazines, 72, 81, 127, 173, 190
Mail, 70–73
Matinees, 90, 172, 173, 174
Mexicans, peach packing by, 119, 121
Mining, 33, 42, 45–47, 62, 101, 188
Minnie (Indian woman), 61, 80, 84
Minniehaha (burro), 23, 25, 27, 28, 53, 60,
    63, 64, 100, 161
    magazine incident and, 73
Mrs. Rose's Grocery and Dry Goods
    Store, 38, 52, 61, 83
Mooney (labor leader), 120–121
Moore's Shipyard, job at, 160
Mount Blitzen, 3, 189, 192
Movies, 126, 174
    influence of, 177
    propaganda, 90, 101–102, 103
    sensational, 172, 173
Mud wagon, 29, 75–79, 80, 86
Music, 32–33, 43, 67, 140, 164
    learning, 126
    popular, 129

Nadine (imaginary friend), 10, 116
Nature, 11, 192
Nemo (chipmunk), 67, 161

Oakland Auditorium, hospital at, 147, 160
Owyhee River, 13, 65

Paiute Indians, 7
Panning, 34, 42–45
Parental conflicts, 40–41, 48–49, 81,
    100–101, 159, 160, 170
    decline in, 184
    noticing, 6, 31–32
Patria, 90, 101–102, 103
Patriotism, 152
    composition about, 103–105
Pavlowa, 90
Peach packing, 117, 119–120, 121
Pedlar, Dolores, 19
Pedlar, Elmer Ellsworth
    death of, 187
    described, 6, 20, 32, 160–161, 162
    first marriage of, 19
    illness for, 179
    letter from, 111
    marriage to, 18–19
    moving and, 2
    poetry and, 36, 78, 151
    reconciliation by, 159
    separation from, 53–54
    shipyard job for, 160, 169–170, 180
    youth of, 19
Pedlar, Etta, 180
Pedlar, Mary Theresa McDonald
    cooking by, 60, 61, 88
    horse accident for, 47–51
    job for, 57, 85, 121–122, 136, 137, 147,
        160
    marriage of, 18–19
    moving and, 1–2
    reconciliation by, 159
    youth of, 17–18
Pedlar, Nadine, 2, 10
Petticoat, incident involving, 155–157
Pickford, Mary, 135, 172
Pie (Paiute Indian), 77, 78, 163
Piggly Wiggly, 185
Pig N' Whistle, 132

Pinkham, Lydia, 41
Pitman, Mrs., 90
Planer, Edward, 181
Plum, Miss, 56, 59, 163
    described, 58
Poetry, 35–36, 75–76, 78
Pony express, 70–71
Porter, Gene Stratton, 67, 90
Prayers, 17, 130
Primeaux, Antoine, 50, 52, 57–58, 61, 82,
    83, 93, 138, 163, 188–190
    meeting, 37–38
    visit from, 91–92
Primeaux, Francis, 84–85, 91, 93
Primeaux, Pat, 38, 52, 61, 91, 92
Primeaux, Roy, 37, 56

Quicksilver, 34, 42, 44, 88
Quong, 35

Rabbits
    cooking, 91
    war on, 106, 107
Rayburn, Miss: dance class and, 186
Reading, 31–32, 40, 67, 174
Real estate business, Agnes and, 182
Records, early, 140
Red (bird), 5, 67, 73, 161
Reed Station, 3, 87
Reeves (Dad's friend), 168
Religion, 11, 130–131
Rest stations, 87
Riggs, Mrs., 160
Riis boys, 184
Roach's Restaurant, 34
Robinson, Ben: squirrel incident and, 25,
    30
Robinson brothers, 25, 27, 101
Roosevelt High School, attending,
    185–186
Rose, Mrs., 38, 52, 61, 83, 84, 163
Rubaiyat, 151, 185
Rum (horse), 77
Russell, Jack, 126

St. John, Al, 135
St. Nicholas Magazine, 31, 72, 190
Saloons, 35–36

Sandy Shore, 7, 8, 22, 23, 50, 54, 67, 83,
    190, 191
San Francisco
    earthquake in, 115
    stories about, 41
    visiting, 126, 127–128
San Francisco Chronicle, 151
Sarah stories, 123
Saturday Evening Post, 72, 161–162, 190
Saturdays, 172–173
School, 40, 53, 56, 60, 80, 88, 148–149,
    174, 185–186
    clothes for, 57–59, 61, 89, 159, 175–176
    flu epidemic and, 171
    starting, 54, 57, 58, 59
Selma
    ranch house at, 116
    staying in, 113–121
    traveling to, 110
Sewell, Anna, 89
Sewing, 32, 132–134
Shaving, 32–33
Smokey (cat), 1, 8, 13, 17, 23, 28, 53–56,
    62, 63, 66, 67, 77, 83, 87–89, 91, 92,
    101, 161
    beavers and, 68–69
    missing, 100, 110, 116
    playing with, 86
    rabies for, 97–98
    removing ticks from, 93–94
    snake encounter and, 14
Snake, 27, 49
    encounter with, 14–15
Snowball (cat), 116, 124–126, 138, 141,
    142, 147, 158, 161, 167, 168, 177
    incident involving, 118
Solitude, 5, 116
    gift of, 192
Songs, 43, 67, 164
    learning, 126
    popular, 129
"Spies" (editorial), 82
Stagecoach, riding on, 86–88
Stage wagon. *See* Mud wagon
Stereoscope, 55
Stokely, Mr., 95, 96, 98
Stories, 31, 101, 123
Street cars, riding, 174–175

Suffragists, 63
  cartoons about, 130

Tereda Mine, 42, 188
Theaters, 127–128
Three Graces, The (picture), 96
Tickets, lying about, 108–109
Toddy (horse), 77
Toothache, problems with, 76–77, 78, 79
Train travel, described, 108–112
Truce (cat), 165–166, 167, 168, 177
True Confessions, 173
Turk Quartz Mine, 42, 188
Tuscarora
  described, 3–4, 34–35
  moving to, 1, 3–5, 52–53, 55
  return to, 78–79, 80, 189, 191, 192
  winter in, 21–22
Tuscarora Saloon, 35
Twin Bridges, 3

U.C. Theater, 125–126
Unions, 117, 120–121
University of California Extension Division, attending, 187
U.P. stores, 185

Valley of the Moon (London), 72, 81
Vaudeville, 126

Wad, The, 8, 9, 10, 50, 55, 89, 101, 116, 151, 192
  self-consciousness about, 123
  weaning from, 22
Weed, Bill, 34
Weed Street, 34–35, 56
Weeks, Margaret: hospital and, 85
Wells, Agnes McDonald, 1, 42, 72, 115, 116, 121–123, 125, 132, 146, 147, 157, 180
  car for, 181
  cat incident and, 118–119

described, 113–114
  letters from, 71
  peach packers and, 120
  poker playing by, 124
  real estate business and, 182
Wells, Patricia, 113, 115, 116–117
  cat incident and, 117–119
Wells, Warren, 113, 115, 116, 117, 122, 125, 135
  car for, 114
  described, 124
  laundry job for, 146–147
  peach packers and, 120
Wells and Bennett, 182
Wells Realtor, 182
West Street, 34
Wheatland Ranch, I.W.W. at, 119–120
White, Pearl, 135
Williford, Alfred, 147
  dinner party for, 131–132, 134–135
Williford, Ann McDonald, 12, 57, 128, 143, 146, 147
  criticism of, 134, 135, 137
  dance lessons and, 140–141
  described, 132
  dinner party for, 131–132, 134–135
  dresses from, 71
  letters from, 71
  living with, 137, 138–139
  petticoat incident and, 155, 156
Will King (automobile), 122, 125, 167
Wilson, Woodrow, 29, 72, 122, 176
  suffragists and, 63
Winter, 21–24, 80
  problems during, 26–29
  transportation during, 70
Wodehouse, P. G., 162
Woman's Home Companion, 72
Words, learning, 10, 31

"Yankee Doodle," 43, 126, 164
Young American Company, 3